I MARRIED YOU

WALTER TROBISCH

A HARPER JUBILEE BOOK

HARPER & ROW

PUBLISHERS

New York, Hagerstown, San Francisco, London

I MARRIED YOU. Copyright © *1971 by Walter Trobisch. All rights reserved. Printed in the United States of America. No part of this book may be used or reproduced in any manner whatsoever without written permission except in the case of brief quotations embodied in critical articles and reviews. For information address Harper & Row, Publishers, Inc., 10 East 53rd Street, New York, N.Y. 10022. Published simultaneously in Canada by Fitzhenry & Whiteside Limited, Toronto.*

First Harper & Row Jubilee edition published in 1975.

LIBRARY OF CONGRESS CATALOG CARD NUMBER: 78-148437

ISBN: 0-06-068449-6

80 81 10 9 8

To three African couples who point the way to the future:

Jean and Ernestine
Roland and Priscilla
Ezra and Gennet

PREFACE

This book is written not only for married persons, but also for those who are preparing for marriage, and even for unmarried persons. Nothing in this book is fiction. All the stories have really happened. All of the conversations have really taken place. The people involved are still living today. For this reason the name of the city is not mentioned nor are any descriptions given. The setting of these events is Africa, but the problems dealt with are relevant to all parts of the earth and to all cultures.

Lichtenberg 6   Walter Trobisch
A-4880 St. Georgen
Austria, Europe

1

THE EARTH came closer. The concrete of the runway appeared. The wheels touched, jumped a little, touched again, rolled. The motor howled. The plane slowed down, turned, taxied toward the airport building, stopped.

I had arrived.

I unfastened my seatbelt, threw my winter coat over my arm, grabbed my hand baggage and struggled down the aisle toward the rear exit.

The African stewardess nodded to me with a smile.

"Good-by, sir. I hope you had a good flight."

"Thank you," I answered, and went carefully down the narrow steps of the landing ramp. I felt the heat like a blow.

Blinded by the bright sun, I joined the other passengers walking toward the airport building.

Halfway between the plane and the building a young girl was standing, looking the passengers over carefully as if she were searching for someone in particular. She wore a stewardess uniform. Suddenly, she took a step in my direction and pronounced my name.

"How did you recognize me?" I said.

"I saw your picture on the back cover of one of your books. I am Miriam. I wrote you a letter once."

Miriam? I searched my memory.

"Did I answer?"

"Yes, you did. You said that a broken engagement is a lesser evil than a divorce."

Now I recalled her letter. I put down my bags and looked at Miriam. She was small, fine-featured, had vivid brown eyes which sparkled below her intelligent forehead. Her long dark hair, almost bluish-black in color, was in a neat roll at the back of her neck.

"You wrote," I said with a smile, "that you were afraid that your feelings for your fiancé were not quite deep enough for marriage."

"And you said I should listen to my feelings. Girls feel it usually sooner than boys."

Now I remembered her case in full. She was a year older than her fiancé, had four more years of education and a better salary than he. That worried her.

"But, you see, I can't just leave him. He loves me and in a way I love him too. Sometimes I don't know how I feel."

"Well, Miriam, we can't talk here. Can we continue as I go through passport control?"

She took one handle of my heavy bag and I took the other handle in my right hand. I tucked my briefcase under my left arm and we started toward the building.

"Excuse me," she said, "but I have to talk to you. When our pastor told us that you would be here only four days, I decided to see you before the others come. I work for the airline. This is why I could come out here."

"Do you belong to Pastor Daniel's church?"

"Yes. He has also come to meet you. You'll see him after you go through customs."

While we were lining up for the passport control, I had the impression that she still wanted to talk. She had made a real effort. It had taken a lot of courage for her to address me, so I didn't want to disappoint her.

"Miriam, I wonder why you got engaged to that young man in the first place before you knew more about him?"

"In our country we can't talk to a boy and go out with him unless we are engaged. We can't have boyfriends. In your book you say one should not get engaged unless one is well acquainted with the other. But we can't get acquainted unless we are engaged."

It was my turn now to show my passport.

"Are you a tourist?" the officer asked me.

"I'm supposed to give some lectures in a church here."

"About what?"

"Marriage."

He gave me a brief glance, then stamped my passport without further comment.

Miriam and I walked over to the place where the checked baggage would be unloaded.

"If I leave him, he said he would commit suicide."

"Suicide? You think he really means that?"

"I don't know, but I'm afraid he does."

"Perhaps it would be good if I could talk to him."

"That would be wonderful. He'll be in church tonight too."

"Then you must introduce him to me after the meeting."

"Thank you," she said with relief. "Thank you very much." From the relieved tone of her voice I concluded that this had been her wish all the time—to arrange a talk between her fiancé and me.

My large suitcase arrived. Miriam spoke to the customs officer in the native language. He waved us on.

The door swung open and we entered the waiting room.

Pastor Daniel stepped forward, grasped both my arms in the African way of greeting, then hugged me.

"Welcome," he said. "You are very welcome indeed."

"Yes, I finally made it," I said, and put down my briefcase.

"I'm glad you're here. May I introduce you to my wife Esther?" He motioned me to a tall, intelligent-looking woman in her middle thirties who stood behind him. Esther wore a dark green dress with a black design and had a yellow scarf on her head. On her left arm she had a baby and at her right hand a little boy, about three years old.

She left him and offered me her hand in the Western way, while looking aside shyly.

"Welcome to our country," she said.

The little boy stared at me curiously. But when I bent over to greet him, he hid behind his mother's skirt, grabbing it with both hands.

"We watched you get off the plane," Daniel said. "We were in the restaurant on the first floor. You started your work exactly one minute after you arrived. Did you know Miriam before?"

"No, I didn't, but we had corresponded. She recognized me from the picture on the back of my book."

Miriam was somewhat embarrassed by this time. She excused herself because she had to go back to work and promised to be at church in the evening.

We walked out to Daniel's car on the parking lot in front of the building. It was a Volkswagen.

His wife got into the back seat with the two children. I sat with Daniel in front.

"How long is it now, since we first met, Daniel?"

"Exactly two years."

I had met Daniel only once and then it was at an international conference for church leaders. He had urged me at that time to come and talk to his congregation. I had not been able to accept his invitation until now.

We drove silently for awhile. Then I tried to tell him how I felt.

"I'm afraid about tonight, Daniel. I feel entirely unprepared. I would like to know a little bit more about the people before I talk to them."

"If you can stay only four days, we have to start tonight."

I could see that.

"Is this the first time you are in our city?" he asked.

"Yes, I'm sorry to say that it is. I've been in other African countries before, but never in your country. I know a little about your customs, but nothing about your particular problems."

"This could also be an advantage," he said with a twinkle in his eyes. "Our young people are looking forward very much to your lectures."

"And the older ones?"

"There is some resistance. They feel that talks about marriage do not belong in the church. Especially sexual matters are taboo to them. I guess it's about the same all over Africa. How is it in America and Europe?"

"Basically it's the same. Christians are embarrassed to talk about sex, and those who do talk about it are very often not Christians."

"Anyway, you should be careful, at least during your first lecture, not to talk too much about sex. And be as simple as possible. Avoid abstract nouns and simplify terms. You'll have to use short sentences, so that I can interpret them sentence by sentence."

"I shall do my best. Do you have a blackboard in church?" I said.

"This can be arranged."

By now we had reached the downtown area. Except for the people, it didn't look too much different from an American or European city—sidewalks, neon signs, tall buildings of banks and insurance companies, hotels, restaurants, travel agencies, supermarkets—and the constant rush of thick traffic.

"Is your family well?" It was Esther.

"Thank you for asking. They are fine."

"How many children do you have?"

"Five, but they are a little bit older than yours."

"Weren't they sad when you left?"

"They wanted to come along. Four of them were born in Africa. They feel this is their home."

"Is your wife going to come?"

"I hope she can join me during the weekend."

"Wonderful!"

I started to think about my wife and how much easier it would be tonight were she along. If only we could speak together. The more I thought of her, the more lonesome I felt.

"We wanted to invite you to stay in our home," Daniel explained. "But we decided instead to put you up in a hotel. It's not very quiet in our home, for we have callers all the time. Also, there may be some people who want to talk to you who would not come to the parsonage."

"I would have liked to stay with you," I answered, "but I can see your point."

"Will you have supper with us tonight?" Esther asked.

"Thanks, Esther, for the invitation, but I'm afraid I have no time. I have to change now. I'm still wearing my winter clothes."

"Well, I just wanted to know. Daniel never tells me when he brings guests home. Nor do I know when he'll be home for meals."

There was a brief strained silence in the car.

We stopped in front of a hotel. Esther stayed in the car with the children, while Daniel accompanied me inside. After I had registered, he followed me to my room. It was a neat-looking single room with bed, desk, and telephone. In front of the window was a living-room area with sofa, armchair, and a small table. The room had a good atmosphere. Here one could have talks.

"I'm sorry I can't pick you up for the meeting," Daniel said, "but I shall send one of our members to bring you to the church."

"I wish you could stay, Daniel, to give me advice on what to say tonight."

Daniel paused for a moment and closed his eyes. Then he looked straight into my face.

"God will give you something. Give us what He gives you." With that he left.

He is a good counselor, I thought. I wished I could help his people as he had helped me now.

I went to the window and gazed out. My room was on the fourth floor, so I could look over the roofs of the neighboring buildings. I had seen them from above, from the plane. Now they were closer, very close. I am under one of them, I thought. Not above, but under.

I took a shower and changed. Then I removed the notes of my first lecture from my briefcase and spread them out on the desk.

I started to read them. But they did not talk.

Suddenly, the telephone rang. It was the hotel switchboard operator. "Just a minute, there's a call for you." A woman's voice came on and asked for my name.

"I read in the paper that you will speak tonight on marriage. Is that right?"

"Yes."

"I would like to ask you a question. Is it always wrong to leave your husband?"

What a question! I thought, and then asked her, "Why do you want to leave him?"

"He won't marry me."

"I thought he was your husband."

"We are living together. He says, 'When you live with me, it's like I married you.' And yet he didn't marry me. He often promises me a wedding, but then he always postpones it. So I am married and I am not married. I am all confused. What makes marriage a marriage?"

"How long have you been living together?"

"For more than a year."

"Do you have children?"

"No, he doesn't want any."

I could just imagine the problems.

"He is very good to me," the voice said. "He pays for my education. He takes me to school in the morning and picks me up at night."

"Takes you to school? How old are you?"

"I'm twenty-two. My parents were not able to give me a good education. So I'm catching up now."

"Where do your parents live?"

"In a small village several hundred miles from here."

"Couldn't you go back to your parents and return only under the condition that a marriage is arranged?"

"That's impossible. My parents threw me out of their house when I started to live with him. They don't approve of him."

"Why not?"

"He's European."

This explained many things: that he had money, didn't want a child, and wanted "free love."

"Well, you really are in a difficult situation. Could you come and see me here in the hotel?"

"No, he wouldn't allow that. He never allows me to go out by myself."

"Why don't you bring him along?"

She laughed. "He would never come."

"Could you come to my lecture tonight?"

"I have classes tonight. Besides, he doesn't want me to go to any church."

"How do you spend your weekends?"

"I stay home. When he goes out, he locks me up in the house."

"Where does he go?"

"I don't know. He never tells me."

I was speechless. Then I heard her voice again.

"But what can I do, Pastor? What can I do?"

The old question. "I don't know," I said, "I really don't."

"Can you at least pray with me?"

"Pray . . . ? Are you a Christian?"

I had hardly asked the question when I regretted it. What would it matter? The answer came.

"No. My parents are Moslem. But I was educated in a Christian school. There was no other school in the village."

Pray! I must admit that I had never prayed over the telephone, let alone with a person I had never seen.

Then I thought, Why not? Did it matter whether I saw and knew her? Did not God see and know her just as He sees and knows me? If we couldn't meet in this hotel room, why couldn't we meet in God?

So I prayed. I said that I had no solution. I asked God to show us a solution. When I said "Amen," she hung up.

The quietness of my room engulfed me. I stared at the lecture notes in front of me and felt helpless. They seemed to have no relationship to life.

Then it came to me with a start that I had forgotten to ask the girl for her name and telephone number. What a mistake! There was no chance to get in touch with her. Would she call back?

The telephone rang again. I picked up the receiver eagerly, hoping it would be she. But it was the operator.

"There's a gentleman in the lobby waiting for you."

"Tell him I'll be right there."

I thrust my notes in my briefcase and went down to meet him. A distinguished-looking man in his thirties wearing a well-tailored suit introduced himself as Maurice. He had come to take me to the church where I was to give my lecture, and led me to his car.

"Are you married?" I asked, as a way of starting conversation.

"No, not yet."

"How old are you?"

"Thirty-four."

Thirty-four and not married. What could be the reason for that? I thought. Then Maurice continued:

"I lost my father in my early childhood. I had to take care of my mother. Besides, I wanted to finish my studies first and have a decent job. I'm business manager for a construction company. Also, it's not easy to find a girl to marry."

"What makes it so difficult?"

"The getting acquainted. I don't know where to meet a girl."

"Do you have one in mind?"

"Yes, I do."

"And what does she say?"

"I don't know. I haven't talked to her yet."

"Why not?"

"The only place I can meet her is in the bus. I know which bus she takes when she goes to school in the morning. I take the same one and try to have a chat with her between two bus stops."

"How old is she?"

"I don't know. Not more than sixteen, I guess."

I gasped. Could this be possible? Here was a fine-looking, distinguished gentleman who had a good job with much responsibility, yet he was pursuing a young schoolgirl in a bus!

"Why do you choose such a young girl?"

"The older ones are either spoiled, or already married. Do you think it's a mistake?"

"Well, you must think that when you are sixty, she will be forty-two."

"Maybe I should think about that."

"Are we going directly to the church? It's quite a long way," I said.

"I made a detour," Maurice answered, "in order to introduce you to one of our greatest problems. Here is our 'red-light district.' "

We had left the downtown area. Hundreds of small mud huts with thatched roofs were on both sides of the unpaved road. There must have been thousands of people living in this area.

"What makes a woman become a prostitute?"

"Many of them are barren women who are sent away by their husbands because they don't have children."

"What makes them barren?"

"The doctors say it is mostly because of venereal diseases which they often get from their husbands who have been infected by prostitutes. It's a vicious circle. Some of them are widows who are trying to make a living in this way so that they can keep their children. If they would remarry they would lose their children to their deceased husband's family."

We drove silently for awhile before we left the district and came to the paved road again. Then we stopped in front of the church.

When we entered, the people were already singing. It was filled to the last pew, men sitting on the left side and women on the right. When Maurice led me down the center aisle, some heads turned curiously, but almost unnoticeably. Daniel was in the first pew and motioned to me to sit beside him.

He gave me a hymnbook and pointed out the stanza they were singing. I could read but not understand the words. But the tune sounded familiar, so I joined in. It felt good to be doing something together with the congregation before I had to address them.

During the last stanza Daniel closed his hymnbook and told me to go first. I mounted the few steps to the pulpit. He followed me and stood by my side so that he could translate.

While they were singing the last line, I had a chance to get an impression of the congregation I was to address. There were quite a few older people filling the front pews. The younger generation, by far in the majority, were sitting more toward the back. They sat close together, their heads with the dense black hair reminding me of a velvet carpet. No one looked up at us.

I whispered to Daniel the passage I was going to read. He opened his Bible. I opened my English Bible.

Then I began.

2

"THERE IS a very meaningful statement about marriage in the Bible. It is simple and clear and yet very deep.

"It is like a deep well filled with clear drinking water. You can lower your pail into it as long as you live and it will never come up empty. You will always draw clear and fresh water.

"If we listen to this statement with an open heart, we will discover that God Himself is speaking to us. He speaks as one who wants to help us. He speaks as one who wants to direct and challenge us. But above all, He speaks as one who wants to offer us something.

"It is the only statement about marriage which is repeated four times in the Bible. The Bible does not speak very often about marriage. Therefore, it is all the more striking that this statement appears four times in very decisive places. First, it sums up the story of creation in the second chapter of Genesis. Then, Jesus quotes this statement in Matthew 19:5 and Mark 10:7, after he is asked about divorce. Finally, the Apostle Paul relates it directly to Jesus Christ in Ephesians 5:31.

"This statement was written about a time which was in many respects similar to ours. It was a time of rapid social change. . . ."

Thus far Daniel had interpreted my lecture sentence by sentence, without hesitation and almost without reflection. It was as if I heard myself speaking in another tongue. But when I used the term "rapid social change" he hesitated for the first time and went into a longer explanation. I continued and tried to describe the time of David and Solomon.

"New trade routes were opening up. Foreign cultures came into contact with each other. New ideas influenced people. Old traditions were no longer practiced. Age-old customs suddenly appeared out of date. Tribes were broken up. Taboos were destroyed. It was a time of complete moral confusion. Everything was plowed-up just as today. Therefore I believe that this statement can serve as a guide for us during these next days. I would like to read it to you now from Genesis 2:24."

Up to this point I had had no reaction from my listeners. But now they started to open their Bibles which many of them had on their laps. I waited a few moments and then read:

" 'Therefore a man leaves his father and his mother and cleaves to his wife, and they become one flesh.' "

As I read it, I was again struck by the simplicity and clarity of this verse. I felt that something was placed in my hands, something to pass on. I continued:

"This verse has three parts. It mentions three things which are essential to marriage: to leave, to cleave, and to become one flesh. Let us take up one after the other. First of all let us talk about

Leaving

"There can be no marriage without leaving. The word 'leaving' indicates that a public and legal act has to take place in order to make marriage a marriage.

"In former times, when the bride left her village for the village of her husband, it was a public procedure.

"Sometimes in Africa the whole wedding party dances, often for many miles, from the village of the bride to the village of the bridegroom. There is nothing secret about it. This public act of leaving makes marriage legal at the same time. From that day on everyone knows—these two are husband and wife, they are under 'wedlock.'

"In our day, this legal act of leaving is replaced in many countries by a public announcement before the wedding, as well as by an official marriage license. The outward form is not of primary importance, but what is important is the fact that a public and legal action takes place.

" 'Therefore a man leaves his father and his mother.' Marriage concerns more than just the two persons who are getting married. Father and mother stand for the family, who are in turn a part of the community and of the state. Marriage is never a private affair. There is no marriage without a wedding. This is why weddings are often celebrated by a great feast.

" 'Leaves his father and his mother.' When I pronounce these words, you will feel a pain in your heart. This is certainly not something joyful. Where I come from tears are often shed when a wedding takes place."

There was a nodding of heads, especially among the older women. Half out loud, one said, "It's the same here."

"You would expect that the teaching about marriage begins with something more joyful and beautiful. But the Bible is very down to earth and sober. It says, 'A man leaves his father and his mother.' Leaving is the price of happiness. There must be a clean and clear cut. Just as a newborn baby cannot grow up unless the umbilical cord is cut, just so marriage cannot grow up and develop so long as no real leaving, no clear separation from one's family, takes place.

"I say, this is hard. It is hard for the children to leave their parents. But it is just as hard for the parents to let their children go.

"Parents can be compared to hens who hatch out ducks' eggs. After they are hatched, the ducklings walk to the pond and swim away. But the hens cannot follow them. They stay on the banks of the pond and cackle."

Even before Daniel had translated the last sentence, there was some laughter in the audience. But it came mostly from the young people.

"You can't get married without leaving," I repeated. "If no real leaving takes place, the marriage will be in trouble. If the young couple have no chance to start their own home, completely separate from their families, the danger is great that the in-laws will interfere continuously.

"In Africa the custom of bride price is sometimes used as such a means of interference. Some parents who do not want to let their daughter go, raise the bride price so high that the young couple remain in debt for a long time. These debts are then used to prevent a real leaving."

There was complete silence in the church now. In that silence I could feel some resistance. I could read in their faces that they were not able to accept this. Evidently this matter of "leaving" was a bitter pill for them to swallow. So I explained:

"Now some of you may say: 'This is against our African traditions. We are taught to love our parents, not to leave them. We feel an obligation not only to the small family—or as it is sometimes called, the intimate family—which is made up of father, mother, and children. We also feel an obligation to the greater family, the extended family, which takes in all our relatives.'

"This is a very valuable tradition, which by no means should be destroyed. Yet my answer is that 'leaving' does not mean to leave in the lurch. Leaving does not mean to abandon one's parents.

"On the contrary, only if a couple are given the chance to leave and to start their own home will they be able to help their respective families later on. Only if they are independent and without debt will they be able to take responsibility for them later on and serve them. The fact that they were able to 'leave' creates a breathing spell in which the love between parents and children can grow and prosper. In my experience, the extended family can function only so long as the nuclear family is intact and healthily independent.

"Is this a Western concept of marriage? It is not. I have not come to you in order to present the Western concept of marriage. I have come to present the biblical concept of marriage. This biblical concept presents a challenge to all cultures.

"Everyone has trouble with 'leaving.' If you ask a Western marriage counselor which problem he has most frequently to deal with, he will probably answer, 'With the mother-in-law problem.' "

There was laughter again—the same kind of laughter and smiles which the mere mentioning of this word causes also in American and European audiences. I continued:

"In America and Europe it is usually the mother of the husband who interferes. She just can't believe that this young girl whom he married is able to take care of her precious son. Will she be able to wash his shirts right? Will she know how much salt he likes in his soup? Even if there is no bride price to pay, money is often used as a means to keep the young couple dependent and to force them to live in the same house or even apartment with one of their parents.

"Real leaving and real letting go—not only outwardly, but also inwardly—is difficult for everyone. In Africa I have heard it is more often the mother of the wife who causes trouble. In case of a marriage quarrel, the young wife tries to run home to her mother.

"So one of my African friends has claimed that this Bible verse should stipulate expressly that a woman shall also leave her father and her mother. Why do African women run home so frequently? The answer is, because the woman has left her family, while her husband has not. In your country the man stays in his home, or close to his home, and his wife has to join him there.

"The man who wrote our verse lived in the same kind of society. There it was a matter of course that the woman had to leave and become a member of her husband's clan. The unheard-of and revolutionary message was that the man also had to leave his family. This must have hurt the ears of the male listeners at that time as much as it may hurt your ears today.

"It protects the women's rights. It aims toward partnership between husband and wife. The message is, in other words: Both have to leave, not only the wife, but also the husband. And just as both have to leave, so also must both cleave—not only the wife to the husband, but also the husband to the wife, as our Bible verse expressly states.

"This leads us to the second part:

Cleaving

"Leaving and cleaving belong together. One describes more the public and legal aspect of marriage, the other more the personal aspect. They are intertwined. You cannot really cleave unless you have left. You cannot really leave unless you have decided to cleave.

"The literal sense of the Hebrew word for 'to cleave' is to stick to, to paste, to be glued to a person. Husband and wife are glued together like two pieces of paper. If you try to separate two pieces of paper which are glued together, you tear them both. If you try to separate husband and wife who cleave together, both are hurt—and in case they have children, the children as well.

"Divorce means to take a saw and to saw apart each child, from head to toe, right through the middle."

A dead silence fell upon the audience.

"Another consequence of this being glued together is that husband and wife are closest to each other, closer than to anything else and to anyone else in the world.

"Closer than to anything else. It is more important than the husband's work or profession, more important than the wife's house cleaning and cooking, or, in case she works, than her profession.

"Closer than to anyone else. It is more important than the husband's friends or the wife's friends, more important than visitors and guests, even more important than the children.

"When I come home from a trip, I always make it a point to embrace my wife first, before embracing my children. I want to show the children also in this way that father is closest to mother and mother is closest to father.

"Very often adultery occurs in a young marriage after the first baby is born. Why? The young wife makes the mistake of becoming closer to her baby than to her husband. The baby becomes the center of her life, which makes the husband feel like an outsider."

From the men's side at least came nodding smiles, showing that they were wholeheartedly in agreement.

" 'To cleave' in this deep sense," I continued, "being glued together, is, of course, only possible between two persons. Our Bible verse was worded purposely as an attack against the polygamy of David and Solomon. It states, 'Therefore a man . . . cleaves to *his wife.*'

"This verse also strikes out against divorce which makes a successive polygamy possible, where one man does not have several wives at the same time, but one after the other.

"Perhaps we would use another word today in place of 'to cleave.' We would no doubt use the word 'to love.' But it is interesting that the Bible does not use this word here.

"Cleaving means love, but love of a special kind. It is love which has made a decision and which is no longer a groping and seeking love. Love which cleaves is mature love, love which has decided to remain faithful—faithful to one person—and to share with this one person one's whole life.

"This leads us to the third part of our verse:

Becoming One Flesh

"This expression describes the physical aspect of marriage."

I remembered that Daniel had cautioned me to be careful about using the word "sex."

"This physical aspect is as essential for marriage as the legal and personal aspect. The physical union between husband and wife is as much within God's will for marriage as is the leaving of the parents and the cleaving to each other.

"I know that some people are embarrassed to talk about the physical aspect of marriage. They feel that it is something unholy, maybe even indecent, something which has nothing to do with God. I would like to ask these people the same question which the Apostle Paul asked the church in Corinth: 'Don't you know that your body is a temple of the Holy Spirit?' And so, we can talk about it. We must talk about it, even in church. I might even ask: Where else could we talk about it, reverently and respectfully, if not in church?"

The silence continued. I realized that these thoughts were completely new for many.

"You say, 'It is against our African tradition to talk about the things of the body. These things are taboo for us.'

"But it is very strange. If I talk to parents in Africa and advise them to teach their children these functions of the body, they say, 'American and European parents may be able to do that, because these things are more natural to them. For Africans this is impossible.' However, when I talk to American and European parents, they say to me, 'Mr. Trobisch, you lived too long in Africa. The people in Africa are closer to nature. They may be able to do this, but for us it is impossible.'

"It is my experience that the embarrassment is worldwide. Parents find it difficult the world over to give their children a proper education about the physical aspects of marriage. The reason is that it has either been considered as something so holy that it cannot even be pronounced—or so unholy that one is ashamed to mention it. The Bible refutes both positions. It says, It belongs to God and therefore we *can*, we *must* talk about it. The physical union of husband and wife is as dear and as near to God as is their faithfulness and the legality of their marriage.

"Of course, 'to become one flesh' means much more than just the physical union. It means that two persons share everything they have, not only their bodies, not only their material possessions, but also their thinking and their feeling, their joy and their suffering, their hopes and their fears, their successes and their failures. 'To become one flesh' means that two persons become completely one with body, soul, and spirit and yet there remain two different persons.

"This is the innermost mystery of marriage. It is hard to understand. Maybe we can't understand it at all. We can only experience it. I once saw it demonstrated in a unique way."

I reached down into my briefcase and brought out a carving of two

heads—the one of a man and the other of a woman. The heads were connected by a chain with wooden links. I held the carving up.

"This is a marriage symbol which the church in Liberia gives to the young couple as a reminder of their marriage vows. If you came close and inspected it carefully, you would see that this chain has no joint. The whole piece of art is carved out of one piece of wood and conveys the message: 'Where God joins, there is no joint.'

"I never found the innermost mystery of marriage more convincingly demonstrated than here. The two become completely one, 'one flesh,' made out of one piece of wood, and still they remain two individual persons. It is not two halves which make one whole, but two whole persons form an entirely new whole. This is to 'become one flesh.'"

I stepped down from the pulpit and gave the marriage symbol to the people in the front row. They passed it on admiringly from hand to hand. I walked over to a big blackboard which Daniel had put up on the opposite side of the pulpit and took a piece of chalk in my hand.

"Now comes the most important message of our Bible verse. We've studied the three parts: to leave, to cleave, and to become one flesh. The message is that these three parts are inseparable from each other. If one of the parts is lacking, the marriage is not complete. Only the one who has 'left' regardless of the consequences, and only those who 'cleave' exclusively to each other, can become 'one flesh.'

"These three elements of leaving, cleaving, and becoming one flesh belong together like the three angles of a triangle."

I turned to the blackboard and drew a large triangle in this way:

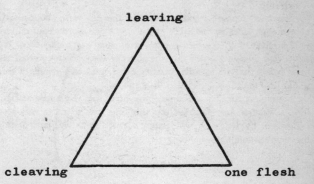

"We could also write at the upper angle, 'public and legal act' or simply 'wedding' or 'wedlock.' At the left angle we could also write 'love' or 'faithfulness.' At the right angle we could also write 'physical union' or simply the word 'sex,' if it is understood that much more is meant by this word than just the sexual fellowship of the couple."

It was the first time that I dared to use the word "sex," but the spirit in the audience was so open by now that I had no need to be afraid of unnecessarily hurting feelings. I said, pointing to the triangle:

"If you want to have a real marriage, these three things have to be in the picture. For young people who are not yet married, this is the goal they have to reach. Just as a triangle is no triangle if one of the angles is lacking, just so marriage is no marriage if one of these three elements is not there.

"But now I have to call your attention to another very important fact about our Bible verse. How does it end? What is the last thing in this verse of Genesis 2:24?"

They opened their Bibles again and hands went up quickly. "It's the word 'flesh,' " an elderly man answered.

"No," I said, "what comes after flesh?"

There was a long silence. Finally, a young man said: "A full stop." There was laughter, but I accepted the answer.

"Yes," I said, "this full stop is of the utmost importance."

I went back into the pulpit and read the Bible verse again: " 'Therefore a man leaves his father and his mother and cleaves to his wife, and they become one flesh. . . .' " Striking my fist on the lectern, I added: " 'Full stop.' "

After a brief pause I continued: "In this key verse about marriage, quoted four times in the Bible, there is not one word about children."

The effect of these words on my audience was tremendous. It was as if I had thrown a bomb into the church. They became restless, shook their heads, started to talk to each other, and some made a certain sound with their lips, indicating disapproval.

"Let me explain!" I called out into the uproar. I glanced at Daniel's face. I was not sure what he was thinking, but he had a very pleased expression. Evidently he was happy about the active participation of his congregation.

Full Stop

I began again:

"Don't misunderstand me. Children are a blessing of God. The Bible emphasizes this over and over again. I have five children myself and am thankful for every one of them. We have received them as a sign of God's goodness, as a very real blessing in our marriage.

"Children are a blessing to marriage, but they are an *additional* blessing to marriage. When God created Adam and Eve, He blessed them and *then* He said to them: 'Be fruitful and multiply' (Gen. 1:28). From the Hebrew text it is clear that this commandment was an additional action to the action of blessing.

"Therefore when the Bible describes the indispensable elements of marriage, it is significant that children are not expressly mentioned. Leaving, cleaving, and becoming one flesh are sufficient. Full stop. Even if there are no children the one-flesh union does not become meaningless.

"The full stop means that the child does not make marriage a marriage. A childless marriage is also a marriage in the full sense of the word.

"The full stop means: Barrenness is no reason for divorce. No man can say: 'This woman hasn't given me a child. Therefore I'm really not married to her,' and then send her away. If a marriage remains childless, this doesn't justify tearing the cleaving elements apart, nor does it question the legality of the marriage."

Daniel had translated these last statements with a special emphasis and with a certain warm concern in his voice, indicating that divorce motivated by childlessness was rather frequent in his country.

And so, although time was running short, I wanted to develop the subject further. I asked Daniel whether I could still go on for ten minutes. He said: "You have caught their ears. You can go on as long as you want." So I continued:

The Garden or the Triangle?

"There is another concept of marriage. It contradicts the biblical concept of marriage which I have just described in every point. This concept of marriage is widespread. I have found it in many parts of the world.

"The garden concept of marriage, as I like to call it, is based on a book called *Marriage East and West* by David and Vera Mace, American marriage counselors, who conducted a marriage seminar with twenty Asians in 1958 at Chiengmai, Thailand.

"This garden concept of marriage as the Maces describe it from China is based on an inaccurate biology.

"It conceives of the man as the sower of the seed and of the woman as the soil, as the garden. Man plants his seed in the woman. The woman's body nurtures the seed as the soil nurtures the grain of rice. Just as the plant grows out of the grain, so the child grows out of the man's seed. The child is the man's child, his ongoing spirit, his continuing life.

"I repeat: This is inaccurate and bad biology. Yet the consequences of this garden way of thinking are tremendous. Let me state them briefly:

"First of all: men are more important than women. The woman can never be so important as the man any more than the soil can be so important as the seed. By her very nature she is secondary, auxiliary. This explains, as nothing else can do, the discrimination between man and woman, not only in Asia, but also in America and Europe even today. Whether it is in Africa, you have to decide for yourselves.

"Second: sons are more important than daughters. It is through sons that the family line is continued. A family who has no sons and whose line dies out is like a tree cut off from its roots. Its ancestors wither and have no peace."

There was a movement among my listeners as if they were deeply involved.

"Third: The relationship between husband and wife is the same as one between a possessor and his possession, just as the sower of the seed owns the soil into which he sows. The main duty of the woman is to obey. It is also the man's privilege to choose. He chooses the garden he is going to buy. The garden has nothing to say. The standard of choice is the potential fertility of the garden.

"Fourth: Within the garden concept of thinking, a childless marriage is as useless and senseless as a barren field. If a woman fails to bear children, she fails in her destiny.

"Fifth: The garden concept explains the practice of divorce and polygamy. If a man's garden does not bear fruit, either he gives the garden back to its former possessor and asks the father of the girl to return the price he has paid for her, or he keeps the garden and acquires one or two other gardens which may bear fruit.* Polygamy is understandable only within the garden concept. Further, man can have several gardens, but a garden can have only one owner. The woman is always at a disadvantage within the garden concept.

"Sixth: I have mentioned the custom of bride price. This custom is closely related to the garden concept. Actually, it is not the price for the garden, but for the fruits which the garden is going to produce. The name is misleading. It is not the price for the bride, but for the children she is supposed to bear. That is why sometimes it is not paid in full until she gives birth to the first child, and then only if the child is a son. A widow loses her children if she marries outside of her late husband's clan which paid for these children. They do not really belong to the widowed mother. By the way, a widow is the most pitiful creature within the garden concept. She is a possession which has lost its owner.

"Seventh: This concept explains why, though both are guilty, a woman is more reproached for adultery than a man. What happens if a man commits adultery? He sows his seed in a garden which does not belong to him. He does wrong to the owner of the other garden and may have to pay him a fine if he is caught. But he is not considered as doing wrong to his own wife or violating his own marriage.

"If a wife commits adultery, however, she does the worst thing she can do to her husband. She allows foreign seed in his garden. She endangers the integrity of his family line. *She* violates her own marriage.

"Finally: There is no place whatsoever within the garden concept for the unmarried person. An unmarried girl is a garden which could bear fruit, but which is not given to a sower. This does not make sense. But the most foolish thing one can think of is a bachelor. He is a sower of seed who does not purchase a garden in which to sow his seed. Unthinkable!"

A roar of laughter followed this last statement. I saw Maurice, who

* The word "polygamy" is used in this book in the sense of polygyny, the marriage of one man to more than one wife. In Africa it is used mostly in this sense because polyandry, the marriage of one woman to more than one husband, is unknown.

had brought me to the church, beaming all over, while his friends slapped him on the shoulder.

"The biblical concept of marriage contradicts the garden concept in every single point.

"First of all, the Bible does away with the inaccurate concept of reproduction.

"It is not out of the man's seed that the child grows, but, according to the Bible and proven by modern science, husband and wife contribute equally to the creation of a new life.

"The child is not only the man's child, but belongs to both husband and wife. Just as *both* have to leave their parents and *both* have to cleave to each other and *both* have to become one flesh, so the child belongs to both husband and wife.

"The garden concept discriminates against women. The biblical concept conceives of the woman not as an inferior being, but as the equal partner of her husband, not an object but a person in her own right.

"The garden concept invites multiple marriages, for it thinks of the woman as a property which can be augmented in numbers at will. The biblical concept aims toward monogamy.

"The choice is between the garden and the triangle. Do you consider your wife a garden or a partner for whom you leave your parents, to whom you cleave and with whom you become one flesh?"

I paused. Complete silence prevailed. Many looked at my drawing of the triangle, and in their eyes I could read one great question. So I continued:

"There is one question left. Where is the place of the child in our triangle? Would someone like to answer this question?"

Many hands went up. I pointed to a woman in her late twenties who had a child on her back. She got up, came to the front, and walked over to the blackboard. Then, without hesitating, she pointed to the center of the triangle.

"Yes," I said, and I could sense a feeling of relief going through the audience. "The place of the child is in the center of the triangle. It begins in the physical union of the father and mother. It is surrounded by the love and faithfulness of both parents, and it is protected and sheltered by the legality of the marriage contract. This is the place of the child in the triangle of marriage. There alone is the atmosphere in which it can mature and be prepared for its own marriage later on."

3

WHILE THE AUDIENCE was singing the closing hymn, I had a terrible feeling of defeat. They had been so silent toward the end. I couldn't resist trying to get an assuring word from Daniel.

"It was too long, wasn't it?" I whispered to him.

"I don't think so. They listened very well."

"But they were so silent at the end."

"When they are moved, our people just become more and more quiet."

But I wasn't sure whether he was just trying to be polite, so I asked him directly:

"What did you think about it? Was it very bad?"

He gave me a knowing smile as if he were familiar himself with the feelings I had, and he said:

"Well, you certainly took the bull by the horns."

"You don't think they were offended?"

"I don't think so. Many things they would not have accepted coming from me, but they will from you. And even if they are offended. What does it matter? It wasn't your message, was it? You must greet the people now."

They filed by one by one, grasping my hand with both hands as was their custom.

Miriam was the last one who shook hands with me.

"May I introduce to you my fiancé? This is Timothy."

A young man in a soldier's uniform stepped forward to greet me. He was rather dark, and although slightly shorter than Miriam, he had a strong, muscular body.

"Thank you very much for your message. I would like to talk to you."

"Why don't you come back with me to the hotel?"

I walked with Miriam and Timothy to Maurice's car.

"What did you think about the lecture?" I asked Miriam.

"I got the message all right. I think Timothy and I are having trouble with the left side of the triangle—the angle of cleaving. We don't know whether our cleaving is strong enough for the leaving."

"All right," I said, "Timothy and I can work on that in our talk together." She seemed to be happy.

Timothy and I got into Maurice's car. While we were driving back to the hotel, I said to Maurice with a smile:

"How is the sower without a garden?"

"Thinking very hard," he said. "It's so true what you said about widows—a property without a proprietor. Exactly. That's why I've always felt and still feel that I have a duty toward my widowed mother. You see, it really wasn't possible for me to leave and that's why I am not yet cleaving."

"And you had no father to buy you a garden."

"No, I had to work for my education and take care of my mother at the same time. I still feel I should continue to support her. If you say that the first condition for marriage is to leave one's mother, I'm afraid I can never get married."

"I said that 'leaving' does not mean to leave in the lurch."

"Yes, I understood that, but how could this be put into practice? If I got married I would have to take my mother into my home. How could I leave her and still have her live with me?"

"There is a difference. If you stay at home and your wife has to move into your mother's home, this usually leads to trouble. But if you move out first and start your own home, then you have actually 'left.'

Then if you offer your mother shelter in your own home, there is much less danger of friction."

We stopped in front of my hotel.

"Well," Maurice said as Timothy and I got out of the car, "all I would need then would be a girl."

"I thought you had one."

"You mean the one I talk to between the two bus stops every day? I don't know. After your lecture I have doubts whether she would be the one with whom I could become 'one flesh' as you interpreted it—sharing everything."

"If you are eighteen years older, she could be your daughter. You would be tempted to treat her like that. In the best case, she would be an obedient garden, not a partner."

Maurice laughed. "I think this is why African men like to marry young girls. They prefer to have obedient gardens. The trouble is, Pastor, I don't know how to make the right approach to a girl, how to talk to her."

"Well, let's talk about that tomorrow. Will you pick me up again? And please bring your mother along."

"My mother? Why, she's in her sixties. I don't think she cares to hear about sex and love."

"Bring her along anyway."

He drove off, and I went with Timothy to my room. We sat down and began talking.

"Miriam spoke to me at the airport this afternoon," I said.

"Yes, I know. Do you think she's a nice girl?"

"She certainly is. Very beautiful too."

"Do you think it would be good for me to marry her?"

"Do you think you can get her to marry you?"

"That's just the point. I know she has her doubts about whether we fit together."

"Did she tell you why she hesitates?"

"No. We talk very little. But I can imagine what it is. I'm half an inch shorter than she is and also quite a bit darker."

"Is that a disadvantage to be darker?"

"Yes, we think it's more beautiful to be lighter."

"Well, Miriam didn't mention that."

"What did she say?"

"I wish that you would ask her yourself."

"But, Pastor, we can't talk about these things. I think Miriam wants you to tell me. That is why she has arranged this meeting."

"I know. Still, it would be better if she would tell you herself. Because in this way you could learn one thing which is indispensable for marriage. That is sharing."

He was silent.

"How old are you?"

"Twenty-two."

"Do you know how old Miriam is?"

"No, she never told me."

"How much does she earn?"

"I never asked her. I left school after I had finished the eighth grade. Then I joined the army."

"What plans do you have now?"

"What do you mean—plans?"

"Well, what are you looking forward to? What are your hopes for the future?"

"Nothing special. After a few years, I may become a sergeant. I don't know what else to say."

"But, Timothy, Miriam has a high school education. She earns more than you do, and she's also a year older."

"Is that so?" he said thoughtfully. "But are these impediments to marriage?"

"Normally not. I could think of bigger ones."

"So you think our marriage could succeed?"

"It could succeed, but not easily. It would take a great deal of effort. It all depends upon whether you love each other enough to make this effort."

"But I love her, Pastor," Timothy said emphatically. "If I can't get her, I don't know what I would do."

"Suicide?"

"I told her that once."

"This is where you made a great mistake, Timothy. It makes me doubt whether you really love her."

"Why?"

"Because you try to force her by menacing her. This isn't love. Love never forces the other one. Real love gives the other one complete freedom, even the freedom to say 'No.' If she married you in order to keep you from committing suicide, she would marry you out of fear, not out of love."

"But what can I do to make her love me?"

"Show her your love. Not by making threats, but by doing some hard work."

"Work?" Timothy seemed to be frightened. "What kind of work?"

"Work at yourself."

He looked at me without understanding.

"You see, Timothy, what worries me about your relationship to Miriam more than your difference in age and education is your lack of ambition. I am sure Miriam wants to make much more out of her life in the future. But you just told me that you may become a sergeant. Maybe. Maybe not. You lack ambition. Should you marry Miriam, this would probably cause trouble."

"But I can't change my height and age, or past education."

"You can change your ambitions, though. Change the things you can change. This would show Miriam more than anything else how much you love her."

Timothy sat in thoughtful silence. I thought he had had enough to think about.

He left, but with a sad look on his face. I am sure he hadn't expected our talk to have such an outcome. After he had gone I realized what a tiring day I had had and lay down for a few minutes' rest. I would have fallen asleep in my street clothes, but the telephone rang.

"This is the girl who called you this afternoon."

"I'm so glad you called again. I forgot to ask you for your name and address this afternoon."

"I didn't want to give you my name and address. I do not want my husband to know that I have such talks."

"Where are you calling from now?"

"From home. My husband just went out for a beer. But when he comes back, I have to hang up immediately."

"I see."

"I was at your lecture tonight. I slipped out of school, but was back before it closed. So my husband didn't notice that I was in church."

"Well, what did you think about my lecture?"

"It was interesting. Only I didn't like your triangle."

"You didn't? What's wrong with it?"

"Nothing, I suppose. I just don't like it. It has too many angles and corners and points. They sting. It's just like a man—what he would think of marriage; all straight lines and corners and everything just so. The pieces must fit exactly together. Very uncomfortable, very unattractive to me."

"Thank you."

"When I think of marriage, I think of something round and smooth and soft. Something you can put around yourself—like a warm cape."

"Maybe I should draw a circle with three sectors."

"I thought of something better. When I looked at the triangle you drew on the blackboard, I thought, It looks almost like a tent."

"A tent?"

"Yes, a tent. It has to have at least three poles, otherwise it can't stand alone. But if it stands, you can crawl into it and you feel sheltered and protected from the storm. It's very cozy in a tent when it rains. That's the way I like to think of marriage."

I had never thought of that. "Do you feel that way in your home?"

"No, I don't. My tent isn't complete. The top corner is lacking: the corner which you called the corner of leaving, the public and legal action of marriage, the wedding."

"If the top is lacking, then it must be raining into your tent."

"Yes, Pastor, it's raining very hard. It isn't cozy at all. Who can help me to repair it?"

She couldn't hide the fact that she was sobbing.

"I would like to try if you will let me."

"But I left my parents and still I'm not publicly and legally married."

"Well, your leaving was a different leaving than the Bible talks about. There was not that mutual and voluntary letting go between parents and child, which in the end binds them that much closer together. You left them out of contempt, and now they have left you in the lurch."

"But why doesn't my husband close the top of the tent?"

"Maybe it's because he knows you can't return to your parents."

"Well, at least he doesn't treat me like a garden."

"What makes you so sure of that?"

"He doesn't want children."

"Maybe he doesn't want you as a vegetable garden, but as a flower garden. Just for amusement in his free time."

"But he didn't buy me. He didn't pay a bride price."

"He pays for your education, though."

"Do you think this is another form of the bride price in order to make me dependent?"

"I can't say before I've talked to him. But it's possible."

"But I love him."

"I know you do. Otherwise you wouldn't call me."

"And he loves me too. That's why he pays for my education."

"I wish you were right. But why doesn't he close the top of the tent and legalize your marriage?"

There was sobbing again.

"Listen, can't you give me your telephone number so that I can call him?"

"Never! He's coming now." She slammed down the receiver.

A tent! She must be a remarkable girl. A tent. Marriage as a tent. I picked up my Bible and turned to the concordance at the back. More than a hundred Bible passages were listed under the word "tent." I looked up several of them, then turned to Jeremiah 10:20:

> *My* tent *is destroyed,*
>   *and all my cords are broken;*
> *my children have gone from me,*
>   *and they are not;*
> *there is no one to spread my* tent *again,*
>   *and to set up my curtains.*

This is her verse, I thought. "No one to spread my tent." If only I knew her name, her telephone number! All I could do now was to pray for her.

It was time for bed. As I took my pajamas out of my suitcase, a note from my wife fell into my hands. I read it: "In love and oneness with you, Deine Ingrid."

My tent, I thought, my tent. Then I fell asleep.

I woke up rather early the next morning and had a good breakfast in the hotel dining room. Daniel came soon after I was back in my room.

He had heard a lot of comments about my lecture.

"How did the older people react?"

"In general, very well. One of the oldest said to me: 'When I first heard that he is going to speak about marriage in church, I thought he must be a wicked man. But now I see that marriage may have something to do with God.' "

"If I got this point across, that's already something."

"You know what I was most happy about? There was a childless couple in church. They suffer a great deal because they don't have children. But they love each other dearly and wouldn't think of divorce. They were deeply comforted that the triangle is complete without a child."

"So the garden concept is very much alive among your people too?"

"Yes, very much so. It's what our people believe right down the line. Also, that the child grows out of the seed of the man, and that sons are more precious than daughters and that the garden must be bought."

It was a pleasure to talk to Daniel. He had deep insights and I'm sure he was the best interpreter I could have wished for. Through him I felt very encouraged. He was a real brother.

"You know, Daniel," I said, "I've almost come to the conclusion that basically there are only two concepts of marriage in the world: the garden concept and the biblical concept, the triangle. Of course there may be all kinds of variations and deviations."

Daniel thought for a moment. Then he said:

"The 'leaving' is the greatest problem here in our city. Our marriages are 'leaving-sick.' Either our children leave without their parents' consent or they don't leave at all. In both cases marriages get into trouble. Our people can't see how you can leave and still remain united, or feel united and leave in spite of that."

"I don't think it can be explained. It is a paradox. The only way to illustrate it is through Christ. In his letter to the Ephesians, Paul says expressly: 'For this reason a man shall leave his father and mother. . . . I take it to mean Christ. . . .' Christ left His father and still remained one with Him. We have a hymn verse in German which translated goes like this:

> " 'The Son goes out from his Father
> and still he remains eternally at home.' "

"All right, but can you explain this to our people?"

"I'll try," I said. "But Daniel, may I ask you a question? What was the point last night that touched you most personally?"

He had his answer ready. "It was being closest to each other, closer than to anyone or anything else. For me it's very difficult to get my work as a pastor into balance with my marriage. I do not have enough time for my wife. My work comes first and she comes second. When she complains that she can never count on me for meals, that is very true. And even during the meal I have to get up three or four times when visitors come or the phone rings."

"I didn't know whether Esther was joking in the car yesterday or whether she was serious."

"She was very serious, Walter. And she is right. But I don't know how to change things. Also, what you said about sharing touched me very much. We don't have that. We don't take time for it."

The telephone started to ring while he was still speaking. It was the girl again.

"Where are you calling from?" I asked.

"From school. We have recess now."

"Did you talk to your husband last night about coming to see me?"

"No."

"I found something for you last night. Do you own a Bible?"

"Yes, I have one from my schooldays in our village."

"Then look up Jeremiah 10:20. It's the verse for you."

"I will. Good-by. The bell is ringing for classes. I just wanted to greet you."

I put down the receiver. "It's my anonymous caller," I said to Daniel. "That's the third time she's called me. She lives with a man who doesn't want to legalize their marriage. But he sends her to school and she takes it as proof that he loves her."

"This is nothing unusual in our city," Daniel said. "It's very seldom that I have a wedding in my church. People hesitate because it makes divorce more difficult. It may be that they will ask for a church wedding when they already have several children. You see, life here is not so straight-lined and clean-cut as your triangle. There are all kinds of in-between."

"Thanks for telling me. That girl did not like the triangle either. She said the corners stung her."

"They stung me all right," Daniel said, laughing.

"Well, let's get back to your problem. Couldn't we have supper together tonight after the lecture when your children are in bed? I'd like to talk with both of you."

When Maurice picked me up that night, an elderly lady was with him. She was small and thin, her hair completely covered with a white head scarf. Out of her wrinkled face, two eyes sparkled.

She greeted me and talked to me as if I understood her language. Maurice translated. "She greets you and says that she is a property without an owner."

"Did your son tell you about the lecture last night?"

She nodded, and pointing to her son, said, "Maurice is an owner without property."

"You have a very fine son."

"He takes care of me very well."

"You can be proud of him."

"But he needs a wife. I would take care of her well. She would not have to do much work. I could cook for both of them."

After Maurice had translated this last statement, I said to him: "She thinks you will bring your wife to her and she will continue to rule the household. You must explain to her very carefully what I said yesterday about 'leaving.' Especially about the kitchen. Even if your mother moved into your home, it must be absolutely clear who rules over the kitchen."

"I wish you would explain that to her," Maurice said. "It would mean more to her coming from you. It's strange, but there are certain things which we accept easier if they come from a stranger."

"I think all people have trouble with the word 'leaving.' It is simply not a human, but a divine wisdom."

We had arrived at the church. It was full again. As I stood in the pulpit beside Daniel, I had a feeling of being completely one with him concerning the message we had to say.

4

"YESTERDAY WE TALKED about the marriage triangle, to leave, to cleave, and to become one flesh which is possible only between two persons.

"Afterwards a lady called me and told me she didn't like the triangle I drew on the blackboard. 'It has too many angles and corners and points. They sting,' she said.

"I understood what she meant. Try not to think of this triangle of wedlock, love, and sex as something unmovable and stiff, but as something alive.

"For instance in a circus, I once saw three jugglers. They stood at equal distance from each other, like three points in a triangle. Each one threw balls to both of his partners and received balls from both of his partners. Each one had to give as well as receive. As long as they were able to keep up the rhythm of giving and receiving, the game went on in perfect harmony.

Interplay of Forces

"Marriage is like this skillful performance. Its life depends upon the interplay between the legal, the personal, and the physical aspects of the relationship." At this point I took a wooden triangle out of my briefcase and held it up for the audience to see. I grasped the bottom left angle and said:

"Marriage needs love. It receives from love its fulfillment, its joy. Love is a gift to marriage. It provides marriage with the spirit of adventure, of never-ending expectation. Love is like the blood pulsing through the veins of marriage. It makes it alive.

"And the state of being married, of wedlock, passes on this life to the sexual togetherness and provides the one-flesh union with a shelter. A woman once told me that she would rather think of the triangle as a tent. Indeed, marriage is a tent for the physical fellowship. The lovers feel protected and sheltered in it. Freed from fear, they experience great satisfaction and a sense of redeemed peace.

"This sense of redeemed peace is then passed on to love. It is the strong foundation in the ups and downs of feelings, of emotions. Within the 'tent' the experience of becoming one flesh strengthens love and makes it grow. It motivates love to faithfulness and makes it want to last.

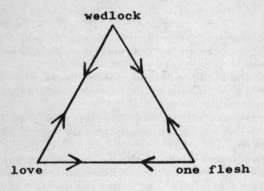

"Love does not only receive strength from the physical fellowship; it also gives the one-flesh union strength. Love longs for the physical expression, deepens it and makes it meaningful and precious. As an act of married love, the one-flesh union becomes an 'act of love' in the full sense of the word.

"Consequently, within the 'tent' the act of love not only receives, but also gives security to marriage. Through the physical surrender to each other, the lovers renew again and again their wedding vow.

"Marriage serves love through this ever-renewed affirmation. For this reason love needs marriage as much as marriage needs love. In the sad hours when love is in danger of growing cold, husband and wife cling to the fact that they are married and remind each other of their mutual promise. 'After all, I married you,' they say. Thus, marriage becomes the protector, the guardian of love.

The Will of God

"In our day there is a great confusion about sex, love, and marriage. This confusion reigns, not only in Africa, but in the East and West as well.

"In the light of this fact our key verse from the Bible appears as a very modern statement. It contains precisely the same three factors. The great question is: What is the will of God concerning sex, love, and marriage? How does God want them to be related? No one dares to answer this question.

"Nevertheless I would like to make a proposition as a guide for our actions in this time of confusion. Here is my proposition:

"God's will is the interplay of forces. Therefore everything that favors it is in accord with the will of God. Everything that hinders it is not in accord with the will of God.

"This guide is applicable before marriage as well as during marriage. Before marriage you will have to ask yourself the question: 'Will what we are going to do prepare us later on for the interplay of forces in our marriage, or will it block us and prevent the interplay?' During marriage, you will have to ask yourself: 'Will this or that action deepen the interplay of forces, or will it eventually disturb it?'

"The interplay of forces within the dynamic triangle is full of elasticity and creative freedom. In Genesis 2:24, God offers us an image which meets the personal need of every situation, every culture. For the will of God is valid not only for the Christian. It is valid for all mankind.

"The dynamic triangle, the guiding image of our Bible verse, is

God's offer to everyone. I say, it is an offer, a gift. God never demands anything from us unless He gives it at the same time."

My audience sat in pondering silence. They looked at the triangle on the blackboard and at the one in my hand. I tried to read their thoughts and said:

"You may feel discouraged now. You may say: 'If marriage is such a work of art, then I am a long way from having a perfect marriage.' I know. I feel the same way. And I know Daniel does too."

Daniel nodded.

"There is no such thing as a perfect marriage. Marriage keeps us humble. The safest way to become humble about one's virtues is to get married. We always have to work on one of the angles of the triangle.

"I would say that most marital troubles point to the fact that one of the three forces is not fully integrated into the triangle. Let us try out our guiding image in diagnosing some marital sicknesses.

"Let's pretend now that you are all marriage doctors. We are going to visit a marriage hospital. Let me introduce you to some of the patients.

"The first patient is one who has had trouble with the left angle of our triangle. Love has grown cold. I call this disease

The Empty Marriage

"Let me describe how this case looks. The couple are married, legally married, and have been for quite some time. They also have had physical fellowship. But love is gone.

"The reasons for this state can be many. Maybe there was no love in the first place. Maybe they married too young and too soon, and what they thought was love lacked the quality of 'cleaving.' Or their marriage was based entirely on physical attraction, and as the years went by, this physical attraction wasn't so strong any more. Or they neglected to put fuel on the fire of their love and became too absorbed by work in household and profession or by the children. They each followed different interests without sharing them, and pretty soon they had lost their common ground.

"It is a dangerous disease. No marriage can take it for a very long time without falling seriously ill. In the beginning this disease can be covered up quite well by the 'married look,' and the outside world is fooled. The couple still inhabit the same dwelling. But that's all.

"The disease does not stand still. As it progresses, these are the symptoms: The partners become cruel to each other in word and in deed. This cruelty on the part of both then gives way to complete indifference and a yawning emptiness in the mutual relationship.

"It is unavoidable that one day this emptiness also affects the physical fellowship. Since the three angles of the triangle are inseparable from each other, the sickness of one will infect the two others. The sex act is experienced as a duty and a burden. A tension is created between sex and marriage.

"Pretty soon the husband looks for a woman who understands him better than his wife. The wife will find a man who can comfort her better than her husband. Jealousy creeps in. Mental unfaithfulness precedes sexual unfaithfulness. Finally, adultery affects the legal foundation and affects the top angle of the triangle also.

"This disease has been described and illustrated in thousands of films and novels. In a false way, these novels and movies put the blame on marriage for the death of love.

"They would like to have us believe that only outside of marriage does love have a chance to live, that only such love is worthy of praise, interesting, attractive, and enticing.

"But the diagnosis is wrong. It is not marriage which causes the death of love, but rather the lack of love which causes the death of marriage. Love outside of marriage, however, easily becomes a destructive prairie fire which, in the end, devours the lovers.

"There is one possibility which is very rarely envisioned by these films and novels. It is the possibility of happy married love, of love as an integral part of the triangle. The true therapy lies here alone. It has to be applied, however, before love dies completely and the other two angles of the triangle are infected.

"Let us go to the next patient, the next couple. Their problem is at the top of the triangle. I call this sickness

The Stolen Marriage

"The symptoms in this case are as follows: The two think they love each other. They also have sexual intercourse with each other. But they are not yet legally married.

"This is one of the greatest temptations of our time: to consider the legal act of the wedding as a mere formality, as an unimportant piece of paper, which one can get someday, or maybe not at all. One pretends that the two angles of love and sex represent the whole of marriage.

"Some people, in all seriousness, propose trial marriages. They suggest that a couple live together for awhile in order to see whether they fit together. If then they come to the conclusion that they do not, they can separate without risking a divorce. But the whole proposition rests upon the illusion that the two angles of sex and love represent the whole. Since they do not, marriage cannot be tested in that way.

"The relationship is sick. The symptoms are as follows: broken hearts and destroyed lives, especially as far as the girl is concerned. I don't know how you feel about it, but in many cultures a girl who has lost her virginity has very little chance of getting married. In our countries, a girl who has had a child out of wedlock is at a great disadvantage. The result is that often a hurried and forced marriage takes place when the girl discovers she's expecting a baby. Many of these marriages end in divorce later on.

"We must consider also the children who grow out of these alliances. They are deprived of the shelteredness of marriage. The top of the tent is gone. It rains in. They are deprived not only of the wholeness of the marriage tent, but also of a father. It's hard to overestimate what this means in the life of a child. Certainly the top of the tent, the wedlock, is essential."

At this point, I couldn't help but think of my anonymous caller. Was she in the audience again this evening? This thought prompted me to add the following remark:

"Those who cut off the top of the tent and practice 'free-love' or 'trial marriages' usually forget to say that this makes the use of contraceptives a necessity. They pretend that this wouldn't have any effect either on the persons who apply them or on their relationship. But this is not true. Especially in premarital situations certain contraceptive methods represent a definite menace to the spontaneity and dignity of love."

Here I hesitated. I didn't know how much I should go into detail. I pointed with my finger at my notes which mentioned "early withdrawal," "heavy petting," "condoms." Daniel glanced at the words and shook his head slightly. This teamwork in the pulpit was a wonderful experience for me. I complied, of course, and continued:

"I repeat: It is a handicap for love. We can make the same observation now which we made before when we studied the case of the empty marriage. If one of the angles of the triangle gets sick, the other two are affected and infected as well. They get into a quarrel with each other.

"When love is lacking, sex and marriage fall apart. If there has been no wedding, then love and sex become hostile to each other.

"The sexual union often takes place hurriedly and secretly under undignified circumstances. Thus the experience does not make love blossom and flower, but makes it wither away.

"We have this problem very often in America and Europe. A recent German film, one of the rare good ones, illustrated very well the disease of stolen marriage. The film showed a young couple living together very happily. After the film had run about twenty minutes, the viewers realized that the couple were not married. Friends and relatives tried to convince them to marry. But they refused. At first everything went all right. Then the girl became pregnant. The love and confidence between them was not deep enough so that she dared to tell her 'husband.' She was afraid that he would leave her. She therefore decided to have an abortion secretly.

"The last scene shows her lying exhausted on the couch in their apartment after the operation. He comes home from work and understands what has happened. He sits down at the other end of a large and empty table which separates them. Silence reigns. Neither one speaks. They have nothing to say to each other any more. Because of the missing angle of the wedding, love has no chance to prove its durability and genuineness. Sex became the death of love."

As I paused for a moment, I sensed a certain reaction among the young people. From the expression in their eyes, I concluded that this film could have been made in their city too.

"Let us go to the next patients in our marriage hospital. There is a third class of marriage diseases. They have to do with the right angle of the triangle. This angle also can fall ill. I would call this sickness

The Unfulfilled Marriage

"First of all, let me describe the situation: The couple is married, legally married, and has been for ten or twenty years already. They love each other dearly and would never think of a divorce. But in spite of this love, their physical fellowship remains unsatisfactory and unfulfilled.

"The husband says: 'My wife is cold. She does not react in the normal way. I feel that she just endures the act of love, but she never invites me. She finds no pleasure in it.'

"The wife says: 'My husband is too quick. I feel that he forces me and abuses me. He never gets enough.' Or she may say just the contrary: 'He's always tired. I am longing, but he turns his back to me and sleeps. I think he is impotent.' "

There was a roar of laughter which I had not expected. I had forgotten in that moment that impotence is a subject of great ridicule in Africa. An impotent man is considered as something less than a human being. An African man fears impotence more than death.

"The diseases of the physical aspect of marriage cause tremendous suffering to the marriage partners. Just because they love each other and would like to make each other happy, they suffer all the more. Where does this disease come from?

"In many cases the unfulfilled marriage is a direct or indirect fruit of the stolen marriage. When I say this, I'm not thinking so much of venereal disease. No, when I say that the stolen marriage often begets unfulfilled marriage, I am thinking of the superficial way of having intercourse with partners who are more or less indifferent, under time pressure and in secrecy, involving only the body but not the heart, not the whole person.

"Again we can observe how the other two angles are affected by this disease.

"When the physical fellowship becomes torture, because it always ends with the disappointment on the part of one or both partners, one or the other will soon reproach his partner for the lack of love. Monotony grows. The personal relationship changes into an impersonal mechanism. Love grows cold. As soon as this happens, the temptation is great to satisfy sexual desire outside of marriage with a more responsive or more considerate partner. Then the legal aspect of marriage is endangered. Adultery and finally divorce are the consequences. This disease, too, may lead to the death of marriage if it is not cured in time."

I gave an inward sigh of relief at this point. So far this had been the touchiest part of my lectures, but Daniel had interpreted without hesitation and the older people hadn't seemed to take offense.

I began again:

"For those who prepare themselves for marriage, the practical question comes up: From which angle do we enter into the marriage triangle?

"In general, there are three answers to this question: a traditional answer, a modern answer, and the biblical answer. Let us take them up one by one.

"The traditional answer proposes entering the triangle at the top angle. I would like to call it

The Wedding Entrance

"Until recent times this was the normal entrance, not only in Africa and Asia, but also in the West.

"The wedding is arranged by the parents and not by the couple. Sometimes the couple see each other for the first time on the wedding day or only shortly before.

"The purpose of this entrance is very clear: It is the child. For what other reason should one enter the triangle, after all, if not for posterity? The wedding entrance belongs to the garden concept."

I picked up my wooden triangle again and pointed to the top angle.

"One enters from the wedding angle and goes directly to the sex angle, or, in this case, we could call it the 'fertility angle,' because the purpose of the sexual union is seen in the narrow sense of producing children.

"The angle of love is left out or very much neglected. It could even be dangerous because it might lead to a conflict between the couple and the family. What if the young people made a different choice from that which the family proposed?

"By no means do I want to maintain that all marriages which are arranged in this traditional way must necessarily become unhappy. Love can certainly grow also during marriage.

"A very popular musical play in America and Europe is called *Fiddler on the Roof.* It tells the story of a Jewish couple, Tevye, the milkman, and his wife, Golde. They are typical of the couples who entered marriage through the wedding entrance. After twenty-five years of marriage, they ask themselves the question whether they love each other. We hear the following dialogue between them:

TEVYE

Golde, I'm asking you a question—
Do you love me?

GOLDE

You're a fool.

TEVYE

I know—

But do you love me?

GOLDE

Do I love you?
For twenty-five years I've washed your clothes,
Cooked your meals, cleaned your house,
Given you children, milked the cow.
After twenty-five years, why talk about
Love right now?

TEVYE

Golde, the first time I met you
Was on our wedding day.
I was scared.

GOLDE

I was shy.

TEVYE

I was nervous.

GOLDE

So was I.

TEVYE

But my father and my mother
Said we'd learn to love each other.
And now I'm asking, Golde,
Do you love me?

GOLDE

I'm your wife.

TEVYE

I know—

But do you love me?

GOLDE
Do I love him?
For twenty-five years I've lived with him.
Fought with him, starved iwth him.
Twenty-five years my bed is his.
If that's not love, what is?

TEVYE
Then you love me?

GOLDE
I suppose I do.

TEVYE
And I suppose I love you, too.

TEVYE *and* **GOLDE**
It doesn't change a thing,
But even so,
After twenty-five years,
*It's nice to know.**

"Americans and Europeans tend to overestimate the value of romantic love. When Africans and Asians warn us about this, we have to listen to them.

"An Indian once compared love with a bowl of soup and marriage with the hot plate of a stove and said: 'You Westerners put a hot bowl on a cold plate and it grows cold slowly. We put a cold bowl on a hot plate and it warms up slowly.'

"There is a lot of truth in this comparison. It does not deny that love is essential for marriage. But it shows also that marriage is more, infinitely more, than just love. It's not only moonlight and roses, but also dishes and diapers.

"Still, in spite of this fact, it remains doubtful whether the wedding entrance is the most promising one. The danger is very real that the power of love never joins the play of forces and thus helps to unfold the dynamism of the triangle. It is, to say the least, a great risk to arrange a wedding without the consent of the partners involved.

* Taken from *Fiddler on the Roof* by Joseph Stein. © 1964 by Joseph Stein. Used by permission of Crown Publishers, Inc.

"I once took part in a discussion group with university girl students at a large African university. The girls wanted to ask questions about marriage. To my great surprise, their most burning question was: 'How can we succeed in *not* getting married?' I asked: 'Why don't you want to get married?' The answer: 'We see so many empty marriages without love all around us that we are frightened at the thought of entering through the wedding entrance.'

"Therefore the modern answer has another proposition to make. It suggests entering from the sex angle and to use therefore

The Sex Entrance

"I would like to make one thing clear at the beginning: when I speak today about those who want to enter into the triangle from the sex entrance, I do not talk about engaged couples. Their problem is a special one and I shall deal with it tomorrow.

"Today I speak about those who start to build their marriage with a sexual experience, because they think that love will grow out of it. Then, as a matter of course, they think that this love will change into faithfulness and from there, almost automatically, finally will lead to the wedding."

I held up my wooden triangle again and pointed first to the angle on the right, the sex angle, from there to the left, and then to the top.

"Or maybe even the other way around. They believe that the sexual surrender will oblige the other one to marry them and then with the marriage license in hand, love will somehow follow.

"Both beliefs are illusionary. Love does not grow out of sex. Love must grow into sex.

"True, within marriage, under the shelter of the tent, sex gives strength to love. But outside of the tent sex is not practiced for love's sake, but for purely egoistic reasons.

"Why does a boy try to sleep with a girl whom he hardly knows and for whom he doesn't really care? Usually there are three major motives:

"1. He is afraid that unless he has sex that he will become sick or neurotic, or both.

"2. He thinks he has to learn by doing.

"3. He wants to brag about his conquest.

"The first reason is not true, the second is not possible, the third is mean, simply mean. None of them comes out of love and concern for the other one. A young man who argues like that thinks of himself only. He uses a girl as a means toward an end, as a tool to reach his own goals. He does not prepare himself for marriage.

"Why would a girl give herself to a boy whom she hardly knows and for whom she does not care?

"Again there are usually three major motives involved:

"1. She wants to be popular with the boys.

"2. Consciously or unconsciously, she wants to know whether she can become a mother.

"3. She wants to bind the boy and provide herself with a husband.

"Again all three motives come out of selfishness and not out of love. A girl who gives herself up for one of these reasons doesn't prepare herself for marriage either.

"She may become popular, but with the wrong kind of boys. Soon she will be known as an 'easy' girl and those who choose her for this reason will certainly make poor husbands.

"She may become pregnant and thus receive the assurance that she can become a mother. But then she has degraded her baby as a means toward an end and it may also have to grow up without a father.

"To bind the boy by sexual intercourse is, in most cases, an illusion. The boy usually loses interest in a conquered fortress. Even if he would marry the girl out of obligation such a marriage has a poor prospect of success.

"A disappointed girl once told me this: 'For me it was the beginning. For him it was the end.' Instead of catching, she lost what she wanted to catch and learned from the bitter experience that sex not only does not make love grow, but that it can destroy it.

"There's a story in the Bible which could be found in any news magazine of our day. It appears in II Samuel 13. The account describes how the king's son, Amnon, seduced his half sister, Tamar. He pretended that he was sick and insisted that Tamar feed him personally. She had to bake little cakes before his very eyes. But baking cakes was not enough. She also had to put them in his mouth—and this only after both were alone in the bedroom. Tamar didn't protest at all.

"Then it happened as it had to happen: 'But when she brought [the cakes] near to him to eat, he took hold of her, and said to her, Come, lie with me' (v. 11). Tamar now tried desperately, at the last moment, to get the wedding angle into the picture. She asked Amnon to get the wedding license from the king.

"But no! 'He would not listen to her; and being stronger than she, he forced her, and lay with her' (v. 14).

"Then we find a statement of tremendous consequence. The next verse reads: 'Then Amnon hated her with very great hatred; so that the hatred with which he hated her was greater than the love with which he had loved her. And Amnon said to her: "Arise, be gone." '

"This story shows us that the marriage triangle is inseparable and indivisible. It is a living demonstration of how sexual desire can become a destroying force which changes love into aversion and hatred when the third angle is cut off and love is not upheld and protected by marriage.

"And so, the one who asks for sexual surrender as a proof of love does not act out of love. When a boy extorts this from a girl with the argument: 'If you love me, then prove it by giving yourself,' there is only one adequate answer: 'Now I know that you do not love me. Otherwise you wouldn't ask for that.'

"It goes without saying that in case a girl uses the same argument and asks to be taken as a proof of love, she deserves the same answer from the boy.

"Dr. Paul Popenoe, the well-known American marriage counselor, has made a very practical suggestion in this regard. He says that a girl should slip a note to her friend which reads: 'Go slowly, my boyfriend, and see all the fine things that are in me. Or go fast, and I shall see how little there is in you.' "

There was a movement of protest among the young men in the audience, so I added: "Since we have a growing number of aggressive girls today, maybe the boys should be prepared to slip a similar note to their girlfriends.

"Let me finish today with the quotation from the letter of a girl, who together with her friend had made up her mind not to enter from the sex entrance.

"She wrote: 'Since we have made this decision there is an easiness in our relationship—the easiness of something not yet final. This is what I appreciate the most. At the same time, there is in this lightness the promise of greatness and depth.' "

5

AS I STOOD at the door greeting the people after the lecture, a rather tall girl whispered as she passed by hurriedly:

"I shall call you tonight at the hotel."

"I'll be at the pastor's home. You must call there."

"All right."

"Tell me your name, so that I will know who you are when you call."

"Fatma."

Then she was gone. Perhaps she is my anonymous caller, I thought instantly. For a moment I was tempted to run after her. But then Miriam came with Timothy.

"Could we have another talk?" she asked.

"I wish you would come together."

"That's what we would like to do."

We arranged a time at five o'clock the next afternoon.

The last ones to greet me were Maurice and his mother. She held my right hand in both of hers, and while she was talking, bowed over and over again.

"She wants to thank you," Maurice explained.

"Ask her what touched her especially this evening."

The mother thought for a moment and then Maurice translated her answer:

"She says that love could enter into marriage later on. And what the woman said in the musical: 'For twenty-five years I've lived with him. . . . If that's not love, what is?'"

I looked at this little old woman with her wiry, worn-out body, looked at the wrinkled face with the lively eyes—and then I couldn't help but put my arms around her and give her a hug.

Just to think she had remembered that line! I was deeply comforted. If she had gotten the message in spite of the different languages, the different cultural backgrounds, then I could be sure that others too had understood.

Different backgrounds? So what! If a line from a modern American musical with a Jewish background, taking place in Russia, touches an almost seventy-year-old widow who grew up in the African bush—the hearts of people must be the same all over the world. The differences are on the surface. Deep down there is nothing but that naked human heart—longing, fearing, hoping—the same wherever it beats.

When I entered Pastor Daniel's house, the table was set for supper. Daniel was still in the churchyard, talking to some of his parishioners. Esther was in the kitchen together with the young girl who was helping her. Esther greeted me and asked me to take my place at the table.

"Supper will be ready in a few minutes."

"Were you in church tonight?"

"Yes, of course."

Evidently she had prepared the meal ahead of time. She must be a very efficient housewife, I thought.

After about ten minutes she put a steaming hot dish of noodles on the table. Then she brought a platter of sliced meat garnished with hard-boiled eggs and tomatoes. A large glass bowl filled with fruit salad —diced bananas, pineapple, papayas, oranges, and grapefruit—stood on the table for dessert.

"Do you prefer tea or coffee?"

"Tea, please. I'm still quite wound up. I'm afraid I couldn't sleep if I would drink coffee this evening."

We sat opposite each other. The place at the end of the table was set for Daniel.

"It must be very tiring to lecture," Esther said politely.

"It's not so much the lecturing, but the talks afterward, which take much strength."

We sat silently for a few minutes.

"Where is Daniel?"

"He's still outside talking to people."

"Doesn't he know that the meal is ready?"

"Yes, he does."

There was silence again. The food was still steaming on the table.

"Can't you call him?"

"It's no use. He won't come until he is finished."

We waited.

"I enjoyed your lecture," Esther said, probably in order to change the subject.

"It is wonderful to have your husband as an interpreter. I feel completely at one with him in spirit, so it's almost as if only one man were speaking. I have a feeling that he improves my lectures quite a bit when translating."

"He does well."

We were silent again. She picked up the hot dish and carried it back to the kitchen.

"You suffer," I said when she returned, "and you are embarrassed because of me."

She struggled with her tears, but then she got hold of herself.

"I love Daniel very much," she said. "But he is not a man of schedule. I don't mind hard work, but I want to plan my day and have order in my duties. He is a man who acts out of the spur of the moment. He is an excellent pastor. People like him very much. But I'm afraid they take advantage of him too."

"Your gifts are different, but they could be used to complement and complete each other."

"Maybe so, but we don't know how to coordinate our gifts. We don't throw the balls into each other's hands. We throw them in two different directions. They fall on the ground. No one to pick them up."

Daniel still did not come. I admired how well Esther mastered her impatience.

"Let me go out to him," I said.

She shrugged her shoulders and tried to smile, but she did not hinder me.

Daniel was standing in the yard between the parsonage and the church surrounded by a group of people having a lively discussion. I said to him:

"Daniel, I have a message for these people. Could you please interpret for me?"

He smiled in agreement.

"Ladies and gentlemen," I said, "this man to whom you have been talking is a very tired man. He is also very hungry. In his house, his wife sits and weeps, because the food is getting cold. Besides that, they have a guest. He is also very tired and hungry, because he lectured tonight in a certain church . . ."

The last words were drowned in laughter and apologies. In less than a minute they all left.

"You can do that," Daniel said as we walked to his house, "but they wouldn't accept it from me."

"Did you ever try?"

We entered the house and sat down at the table. Esther brought the hot dish in from the kitchen again. Daniel said grace. Then the telephone rang. As if stung by a bee, Daniel jumped up.

So did I. I put my hands on his shoulders and forced him back in his chair, telling Esther:

"You go and take it! Tell the caller that your husband is having his evening meal. Ask whether he could call him back later on or whether you could take a message."

She came back quickly. "It was a man. He said he just wanted to greet you. He had no special reason for calling."

We began our meal together.

"It's always the same," Esther commented. "As soon as we sit down for a meal, the telephone rings. Daniel gets up four or five times during each meal."

"You will get sick, Daniel, if you continue like this. And Esther, it's your duty to protect him."

"If only he would let me."

"Daniel, you're not the bellboy of your parish, you are the pastor."

The telephone rang again. I realized that it took all of Daniel's strength and will power not to get up. I nodded to Esther and she went to answer it.

While she was away, Daniel said:

"You see now why we put you up in a hotel?"

"Yes, I understand. But you must find a solution. This is bad stewardship of your time and strength."

Esther returned. "Someone's mother is sick," she said. "But it's not serious. I could see her tomorrow morning. I took the address down."

"Really, Esther, you shouldn't have to answer the telephone either. You should train someone from your parish to take these calls at certain times."

"It's not only the telephone. The visitors and callers too are a problem. They come at any time."

"I can see no other solution. You must decide on certain hours when you are available and then post these times on the door."

Daniel said, "Africans wouldn't understand it. They would think it is very impolite. It is against their traditions."

"Listen, my brother, if you would come to Germany and I would take you to any local parish, I can promise you that the pastor there has the same problem. It's a question of whether you are obedient to your customs or to your calling. You know the story about the lighthouse keeper. It was his responsibility to keep the light burning and supplied with oil night and day. The lighthouse guided ships as they passed through a dangerous strait. The people of the nearby village would come to the lighthouse keeper and would ask him for just a little bit of oil for their lamps. He was too good-natured ever to say 'no.' So he gave away his supply of oil little by little. One day there was no oil left and the light went out. A ship went on the rocks and sunk. His good-naturedness had caused the death of many."

"You are right," Daniel said. "I just can't say 'no.'"

"It's not only your ministry which is at stake, but also your marriage."

"We have to make a new start, I know. It's the right angle of the triangle which we need to work on—the angle of sharing."

"If we could only have fifteen uninterrupted minutes together every morning!" Esther said. "But we stumble into our day without a plan and then we just wait and see what happens. I never know what he is going to do. He doesn't know what I do. We have no fixed mealtimes. It's hard on the children too."

There was a knock at the door. Both of them looked at me inquiringly.

"What is the girl in the kitchen doing?" I asked.

"She is waiting to wash the dishes when we are finished."

We heard the knock again.

"Tell her to go to the door and tell the caller to come back tomorrow—"

"But it must be before nine o'cock," Daniel interrupted.

After a few moments the girl returned.

"What did he say?"

"He agreed."

"Well," Daniel said, shaking his head, "in the long run, our people will not understand this."

"If you never challenge them, of course they won't. This quarter of an hour in the morning which Esther asks for is like the rudder of the day. Don't forget: the testimony which you give with your own married life does more than a hundred lectures on marriage!"

Daniel replied: "I tell you that we have to remind ourselves many times that we are married. If it were just for our feelings of love, our marriage would have been on the rocks long ago."

"And this in spite of the fact that we love each other," Esther interjected. "I love him very much and I know he loves me."

"It's not in spite of the fact that you love each other," I said, "it's because of this fact that you have to remind yourselves that you are married."

"Is this idea, that marriage upholds love, generally accepted in America and Europe?" Daniel inquired.

I'm always a little afraid when Africans begin asking me these questions.

"Not at all," I said honestly. "In America and Europe today the triangle is very torn apart. Marriage and love are torn apart; love and sex are torn apart; and, of course, sex and marriage."

"How do they tear love and marriage apart?"

"With the argument that 'love' justifies everything. With or without marriage, you may have sex wherever you want, whenever you want, and with whomever you want—as long as you 'love' him or her."

"And what is wrong with this thinking?"

"It is unrealistic. They do not see this world as it is. There is no such thing as unlimited freedom. Just like a forest or prairie fire becomes destructive, so does 'free love' become inhuman, demonic. The Soviet Union tried at one time to set love free in that country. The experiment ended in failure. Marriage means for love what the hearth means for fire."

"But how can I explain this to my people?"

"There is only one way: through God's love. God Himself is love, but He gave up His freedom and power. He humbled Himself and accepted restraint and limitations. God became incarnate. Love was made flesh."

"But that would mean that only the one who believes in the God incarnate can help people with their marriage problems."

"In the deepest sense, yes, because only he knows that God Himself is hidden in the one we love. Unless we encounter God in our partner, we fail our partner."

Daniel thought for awhile.

"And how do they tear love and sex apart in the West?"

"There are, of course, many opinions. A certain trend of thinking pleads for sex without love. These people would ridicule love as chitchat. They would say, 'Sex is for fun, not for love. For sex, love is repressive. Sex is for the happiness of the moment. It's a pleasure only if practiced without obligation and without regret.' But Daniel, my brother, I didn't come to talk to your people as a Westerner. I came as one who believes in the God incarnate."

"I know that. Otherwise I wouldn't have invited you," Daniel said warmly. "But are you saying that this message would be still less popular in America and Europe today than it is in Africa?"

"Precisely. Whoever proclaims the message of the dynamic triangle is a lonesome voice in the wilderness, regardless of the culture. The one who formulated this verse—that a man shall leave his father and mother, cleave to his wife and become one flesh with her—must have been a lonesome person too. It strikes me that no one else in the Old Testament quotes this verse. None of the prophets—until Jesus uses it."

"But isn't a certain garden concept also present in the Old Testament?" Esther asked. "There is male dominance. There is divorce as a man's right. There is polygamy and emphasis on fertility."

"I think it's a process, Esther," I replied. "I think that the message of this verse started a process which permeated the Israelitic culture. There is also a trend in the Old Testament to overcome the 'garden concept.' When Jesus quotes this verse in the New Testament, he uses it clearly against divorce and in favor of monogamy."

The telephone rang again. Daniel waved his hand to his wife with the gesture of an Arab sheik. "I'll let my garden serve me," he joked.

Esther got up obediently and went to Daniel's office, where the telephone was. She came back laughing and addressed me:

"This time it's for you."

Before I could catch myself, I jumped up just as Daniel had done earlier. Daniel roared with laughter while I stood in embarrassment, realizing that I had acted against my own advice.

"You are excused," he said graciously. "First of all, except for half of your dessert, you have finished the meal. Second, you have shown me that you are not a legalist."

I picked up the receiver.

"Is this Fatma?"

"Yes."

"Tell me, are you the one who called me already twice yesterday?"

"Yes, I'm the one."

"Then at least I now know your name."

"Is that important?"

"It's easier to pray for you."

"Do you pray for me?"

"Yes."

"Why do you do that?"

"It's the only way I can help you. Humanly, I am at my wit's end. Besides, you asked me to do it once."

Silence.

"You were in church again tonight?"

"Yes."

"Without permission again?"

"Yes."

"Did you hear that I used your idea of the tent in my lecture?"

"Yes, I did. And I looked up the Bible verse you gave me. It certainly is the verse for me: 'My tent is destroyed, and all my cords are broken.' All of them, Pastor. After hearing your lecture tonight, I know that they are all broken. It's so true, what you said."

"What do you mean?"

"About contraceptives being a threat to love."

"Well, I was wondering all the time how you solved that problem."

"We haven't. That's just it. He may think he has. But for me it isn't solved. First he told me to watch the fertile days and count them on the calendar. But this didn't work and I became pregnant. He told me to abort my child."

"And you obeyed him?"

"Yes, of course. Now he makes me swallow a pill every morning. But that means that after three weeks, I have a week of bleeding. And I have no pleasure. Especially since I've been taking the pills, I feel almost numb."

"Many women who take pills say this."

"Are contraceptives bad, Pastor?"

What questions she asks! "You see, Fatma, it all depends upon whether the tent is broken down or whether it's intact, whether it's whole. If the tent is whole, husband and wife can talk together in confidence. For a certain reason they may decide not to have a baby, or to wait to have another baby. Then they will agree about the method, usually with the help of a doctor who can also supervise them medically. They will be frank with each other and tell each other how they feel. Even if a pregnancy should come sooner than they had planned, this would be no disaster. Since the tent is whole there is also a sheltered place in it for the baby. Everyone needs a place, even a baby. But if the tent is broken down, if one of the poles is missing and it rains in, then everything is different."

"I know that only too well. I'm terribly afraid of another pregnancy, because then he would force me to have another abortion. It's exactly as you said, if one corner is lacking, the two others don't work. As the Bible says, 'There is no one to spread my tent.' "

"Listen, Fatma. It's no use to go on making complaints over the telephone. If you want things to change, you must bring your husband to me so that I can talk to him."

"Impossible!"

"Try it anyway."

"Should he come alone, or should we come together?"

"As he prefers."

"He's coming home now. We have to stop. Good-by, Pastor. Thank you."

When I returned to the table I told Daniel and Esther something about Fatma's problem in hopes that they would be able to help.

"He really treats her like a slave," Esther commented.

"We have to face it," Daniel added. "The matter of absolute male dominance is deeply engrained in African culture."

"Esther and Daniel," I said, "I'm ashamed to admit it, but Fatma does not live with an African. The man with whom she lives is European. It is not a question of culture. It is a question of the human heart which the Bible calls deceitful."

They said nothing. Sensitive to the feelings of others, they were saddened because of my embarrassment.

"Tell me, Daniel, if she decides to leave him, to take a job and live alone—would this be possible?"

"Not in this city. It's as good as impossible. We still live very much in the garden concept. There's no place for a single person."

"Then he has her entirely in his power. Her parents slammed the door behind her when she left with him. Another man wouldn't marry her now because she's no longer a virgin. And living alone is impossible. She is right. There is no one to spread her tent."

"In any case, she has to leave him," Daniel said. "Maybe she could move in with some relatives or friends. But suppose she actually were married to him. Do you advise people sometimes to get a divorce?"

"Would a doctor advise his patient to die? He would fight for his patient's life as long as there is a spark of hope. In the same way I would fight for a marriage as long as there is the least sign of life in it. But there are marriages where you simply have to admit: This marriage is dead."

"I can think of marriages where love has died completely," Daniel said. "The physical union has ceased long ago. All the husband and wife have left is the top angle of your triangle. They are married. The rest is gone. They may still live in the same house, but they go different ways. Mostly they live separated lives. Still they are not yet divorced. This goes on for years. To me such a marriage is dead. Still, Jesus has said: 'What God therefore has joined together, let no man put asunder.'"

"But the question is: 'Did God join them together in the first place?'"

"Would you remarry divorcees then without hesitation?"

"Not without hesitation. With much hesitation. But under certain conditions I would. In any case, I would remarry only the guilty party."

"I don't follow you."

"If someone claims that he is entirely innocent when his marriage has failed and that the fault is one hundred per cent his partner's, then I know that his second marriage will be a failure too."

"But there are people who really are innocent. Take the case of the husband who becomes a drunkard."

"Yes, but beneath this surface innocence there is a deeper level of guilt. On this deeper level, man stands not before his partner, but before God. This deeper level of guilt often has to do with the way in which the marriage came into being. I would hesitate to remarry anyone before he is ready to face this deeper level."

"Is Fatma innocent?"

"Of course, her parents are very much at fault. And then this man, too. Yet, before God, she is not innocent."

"How do you think you can help her?"

"I don't think I can help her at all until she realizes this."

I had been talking with Daniel alone about this question. Esther had sat down in an armchair to drink her tea. When we looked at her, we saw she was asleep.

"My garden went to sleep," Daniel joked.

"She's not your garden, Daniel. She's your roommate in your tent—your tentmate, if you want to put it that way. You need some sleep yourself. Could you take me back to my hotel?"

When I picked up my key at the hotel desk, the clerk handed me a letter. It was from my wife. I went up to my room, sat down and read:

"How I miss you and being able to talk things over with you. The whole past year has been one separation after another. I actually believe that we have not had one single quiet week together at home this year. Either we were trying to meet some deadline or getting ready for some trip. We had so little time to just live.

"This afternoon I saw the windows of a house high on the mountain flame in gold as the setting sun touched them. The reflection almost blinded me.

"I thought, this is the way it is when we are quiet and let Christ be reflected through the windows of our soul. And I thought, This is the way it is when I can be completely one with you in body, mind, and soul. There is a certain transfiguration. Because I have tasted this joy, I long for it. It gives me the strength to overcome all the demands of our daily living.

"This experience of complete oneness was withheld between your last trip and this new one. My heart grew heavier and heavier, so that I could hardly bear it. That's why it was so hard to let you go this time.

"So when you are working, please know that all these hopes and desires which cannot be separated from my heart and soul are also in this work. They are a kind of burnt offering which makes the time more fruitful, not only for you, but also for your wife.

"This is not a letter of complaint. It is simply sharing a fact. For me this sharing means that I can go forward with a lighter heart.

"Thanks for always listening. Now I can go forward again. I can hardly wait to join you Saturday."

What had I said in my lecture? "There is no such thing as a perfect marriage. Marriage keeps us humble. The safest way to become humble about one's virtues is to get married."

I was still fast asleep when a ringing sound wakened me. As I struggled out of bed to turn off the alarm, I realized that the ringing was from the telephone.

I turned on the light. It was 2:00 a.m. I picked up the receiver. The night clerk apologized for waking me up.

"There's a couple here in the lobby. They insist on seeing you."

Wondering if it could possibly be Fatma and her "husband," I asked the clerk to wait five minutes before sending them up. I would receive them as soon as I was dressed.

I have seen many beautiful African girls, but never anyone like Fatma. She was tall and slender and wore a national gown which went down to her ankles. She walked with grace, but with a certain restraint. Everything was neat and clean about her. She had selected her necklace, earrings, and bracelet, which set off her fine-featured face, with distinctive taste. Her large brown eyes had an air of sadness about them.

The man who was with her wore his working pants, partly torn and spotted with oil. His T-shirt was not tucked in at the waist. He was unshaved and had dirty fingernails. He was blond.

After Fatma had introduced her companion, she was full of apology because of the impossible time of their visit. She said they had argued until 1:30 when he finally gave in and was ready to come and see me together with her.

"If we hadn't come right away, he might have changed his mind."

"It doesn't matter, Fatma. I'm very glad you came, both of you." I addressed myself to him: "I'm especially glad that you came with her, sir. It shows me your concern for Fatma, Mr.—"

"Call him John," Fatma said. "It's not his real name, but it's the English equivalent of it."

John had slumped down in the armchair and sat there with outstretched legs, his arms folded across his chest. He was hostile and I wasn't surprised. Of course, he was afraid of me and naturally suspected that I was on Fatma's side. It was a difficult situation, for I had to admit to myself that I was on her side.

"You must be terribly afraid of me."—No reaction. "Probably you think that Fatma has accused you. But she never did."—No answer. "She told me that you take good care of her. She is very thankful to you, especially that you send her to school. I see also that you enable her to dress nicely."

He shrugged his shoulders.

Fatma said: "You are very good to me, John. I don't know what I would do without you. I am thankful to you. I love you very much. But I can't understand why we don't get married."

"The old story," he said with a sigh, and without looking up. "Why do we need that paper? There are hundreds of couples in my country who live without that paper and who are happy. There are others who have it and who are unhappy. It's not the paper that makes you happy."

"But I am ashamed when I meet one of my friends. What shall I tell them? Am I married or not?"

"Your friends! I'm not interested in your friends."

"But they are a part of me. If you love me, then you must love me with my friends.—For me, it's not the paper, but the wedding feast which is important. I would like to have a real feast and invite three or four hundred people."

He threw up his arms in horror. "Three hundred people!" he exclaimed. "I tell you, *if* we get married, then it will be a very small wedding. Just the two of us and the witnesses in the City Hall. That's all!"

"But then in our country, everyone would think I was ashamed of you, that I am hiding something. I want to show the people that I am proud of you. I couldn't stand the shame of a small wedding."

There was silence.

"My impression is, John," I said carefully, "that you have taken a step, but that you are not yet fully aware of all the consequences."

"What step have I taken?" he asked in a snippy way, but I was glad that he had at least started to talk to me.

"Of taking Fatma into your house. You see, if you choose a girl in this country as your wife, or would-be wife, you do not choose just this individual person, isolated from everything else. You choose her with her education, her tastes, her likes and dislikes, her habits and customs, in short, with her culture. From this short conversation which we have had, I conclude that you might love her as an individual, her beauty and character, but you don't love her with her culture."

"I love her," he said in a stubborn, defensive tone.

"Yes, I understand. But real love means to love her with her background, her culture. A big wedding feast belongs to this culture. If you marry a girl from this country, then you must accept this fact. More than that—you must not only accept it ungrudgingly, you must even like it."

He was silent again. My impression was that these thoughts were new to him.

"You see," I continued, "marriage is a burden, a responsibility, even under normal circumstances. This additional burden of cultural differences is often the straw that breaks the camel's back. What makes these marriages break down is the fact that the partners do not fully accept each other's different cultures. This may start with tiny things, such as the likes and dislikes of certain foods or the way of preparing them— and it may end with a different outlook on life as a whole."

"Do all these marriages fail?" Fatma wanted to know.

"No," I said. "But if they succeed, it is usually because both have lived for a long time in the culture where they plan to make their home.

"Unfortunately, this is very rarely the case. If an African student marries an American or European girl, whom he meets in her country and who has never been in Africa before, their marriage almost always fails. In spite of her goodwill and sincere desire, she is unable to make the adjustment."

"She takes a step bigger than his pants allow," John joked, and then laughed at his own joke. I was glad that he seemed more relaxed now and so I dared to say:

"There's a possibility that both of you are in the process of making the same mistake."

"We love each other," John insisted. He looked to me like a little boy afraid that someone would take away his toy.

"Yes, but marriage is more than love. 'It's not only moonlight and roses, but also dishes and diapers.' "

"Diapers!" John turned up his nose in distaste.

"You don't like children?"

He shook his head.

"How about you, Fatma?"

"I love them very much and I want to have many."

"Another point where you disagree," I observed, "and a rather important one. What are your plans, John? Do you plan to stay in this country?"

"I have a job with the government, but my contract expires in a year."

"And then?"

"I don't know. I may go someplace else—like South America or Japan."

Fatma gasped.

"I take it that you want to take Fatma along."

"What makes you think that?"

"Because you said that you belong to the husbands who are happy without a paper. If one is really happy, one doesn't want to give up one's happiness."

He shrugged his shoulders. Then Fatma exploded.

"You never told me that your contract expired. I always thought that you wanted to stay in my country all your life."

John suddenly got up.

"Good-by. We have to go now. It's getting late—or rather, early."

"Just one word," I replied, taking his hand and looking him straight in the eye. "Please, John, for Fatma's sake, make up your mind. If you want to take her along, then tell her so, so that she can make a decision. If you don't, and plan to separate after your contract expires, then tell her, so that she can make up her mind whether she wants to stay with you. I'm not telling either one of you what to do, but I plead with you, stop playing hide-and-seek and make up your mind."

"Thank you very much," he said coolly.

"Do you have far to go?" I said in order to release the tension.

"No, just across the river."

Then he left the room. Fatma trailed after him without looking at me.

I went back to bed, but I couldn't really go back to sleep. My thoughts wouldn't settle down. The people kept walking through my mind: Fatma and John, Miriam and Timothy, Maurice and his mother, Daniel and Esther—my wife.

I got up and ordered an early breakfast in my room. Then I read my wife's letter again. Why couldn't she have written a more encouraging letter? "How I miss you and being able to talk things over. . . ." Hadn't we done that all the time? After all, our separation isn't long this time. Is that really so difficult?

I made an attempt to read, but my thoughts returned to my wife.

Why does she write such a letter? She wants me to comfort her, I thought. Why am I so disappointed? I feel that she doesn't understand me, my work with all these problems I can't solve, with all these people I can't help.

Since I don't feel understood, I can't comfort her, I thought. Since she is not comforted, she can't understand me. A vicious circle.

"Thanks for always listening. . . ." Was I? Was I really? At least she was talking. Wasn't she doing what Fatma and John could not do —not even Timothy and Miriam—nor Daniel and Esther either? Yes. The thought helped me. We still were talking in our tent, even if it were sagging.

I opened my Bible and read the 27th Psalm. I drank it in—every word of it—like a fresh, cool drink of water.

"Though a host encamp against me, my heart shall not fear; . . . for . . . he will conceal me under the cover of his tent."

These words had never touched me before. They had never had any special meaning for me. Suddenly they talked, talked with a thundering voice.

His tent, I thought. It's not our tent, it's God's tent. We are in His tent. His tent is not sagging.

After breakfast the telephone rang. It was Fatma again.

"From where are you calling?"

"From home."

"Why aren't you at school?"

"He said I should sleep this morning. He was very considerate— more than he has ever been before."

"Did he lock the house again?"

"Yes, he is very jealous. Isn't jealousy also a sign of love?"

"Of a certain kind of love. A very possessive kind, not very mature. Mature love has confidence and grants the partner freedom."

"Do you think he has no confidence in me?"

"What do you think?"

She evaded the answer and changed the subject.

"The reason I'm calling is I would like to know what you think of him."

"He came so unkempt and I wondered if he had even washed his hands. Doesn't his appearance bother you sometimes?"

"Yes, but I think that love must be able to overcome this. And I love him and he loves me."

She is clinging to a straw, I thought. Hadn't the talk early this morning opened her eyes?

"Yes, Fatma, maybe. But you are thinking of different things when you say to each other, 'I love you.' He thinks of sex, while you think of marriage. That's the difference. You aren't putting up a tent. You have one pole in the ground, or you think you have—your love. But then he puts one pole on the right of it and you one pole on the left of it. It will never hold up a tent."

"What do you think his plans are?"

"He doesn't want to make up his mind. This is what makes the situation so difficult for you."

"Do you think he will leave me after his contract has expired?"

It was evident that she hadn't caught on to his remarks. Unbelievable! The least I can do for her, I thought, is to let the light in so that she can see.

"There is nothing that can force him to marry you, nothing that can hinder him from leaving you."

Silence.

"And to be frank, I almost wish he would leave you. You wouldn't become happy with him."

I felt, as I was speaking, that these words were cutting her like a knife.

"But if he leaves me . . . there is nothing. There is an abyss. Where shall I go?"

Into God's tent, I thought. If only I could lead her to it. If only I could heal after cutting.

She didn't hide her crying now. Her voice drowned in sobs.

"Good-by, Pastor," she said.

"Fatma," I called, "read Psalm 27. There is a message in it for you." I wasn't sure whether she had hung up before I could say that.

Miriam and Timothy came late that afternoon. It was almost 5:30. They explained that Timothy had been unable to leave sooner.

"Well," I said, "then we have to get right to the point, for Maurice is coming soon to pick me up. What worries me the most about your relationship is the fact that you are evidently not able to talk together. Timothy didn't even know how old you were, Miriam, nor how much education you have had, nor how much you earn. Actually, I knew more about you than Timothy did. How do you explain that?"

"We had a short talk before we came here," Miriam said, "and we too want to get right to the point."

It was interesting that she did the answering.

"We have entered our triangle from the sex entrance," she continued. There was a brief silence. I realized that it took a lot of courage for her to say that. I liked her honesty. "I told you that in our culture we can't meet unless we are engaged. But then about four weeks after our engagement we became intimate."

"What does this have to do with your inability to talk together?"

"Very much. It soon became the main thing, the main reason for our dates. We knew that when we met we would end up uniting. We thought just of this one thing. Everything else became secondary."

"But now, Timothy and Miriam, you must explain something to me so that I can better understand. You say that in your culture, you can't meet unless you are engaged. Does it also belong to your culture to become intimate during the time of engagement?"

"Well," Timothy said with a smile, and somewhat embarrassed, "you see, we belong to the younger generation. We young people of today are more modern. We stand for progress. We don't consider the old traditions binding any more."

"That's just what I wanted to hear," I said. "As long as your customs meet with your own desires, you are 'African' and you don't hesitate to get engaged, without even knowing each other. But if your customs do not comply with your desires, suddenly you become 'modern' and 'progressive' and throw your customs overboard.

"In German we say it is like someone who wants to drill a hole in a board of varying thickness, but he always chooses the place where it is thinnest. Am I too hard on you?"

"Please be hard," Miriam said. "I wished our parents would have talked so hard to us. But they never talk. They just suspect."

"All right, then let me be hard. First you say, 'In our society it is impossible for young people of different sexes to meet. We can't even talk together, unless we are engaged.' Then all of a sudden you find it possible to sleep together in spite of all the social restrictions. Why should it be so hard to talk together and so easy to sleep together?"

They looked down at the floor. Finally Miriam said:

"It isn't easy. The only place we could find was in a car."

"It was the only place," Timothy said. "Her family is very strict, and mine too."

"Yet you found a place in spite of their strictness," I said. "If you really wanted to, you could also have found a place to talk even without being engaged."

"But Pastor," Timothy said, "I don't regret it. It's not true what you said yesterday that sex without marriage destroys love and makes it change into hatred. At least in our case it isn't true. It deepened our love. It was beautiful."

I looked at Miriam. She grasped Timothy's hand as if she didn't want to hurt him. Then she said softly:

"Maybe it was for you, but for me it wasn't."

"It wasn't?" Timothy seemed very surprised. "What exactly wasn't?"

"Everything. The place. The hurry. The secrecy. The fear of being discovered. A car isn't exactly a tent in which you feel sheltered."

Timothy drew a heavy sigh. A world broke down for him.

Miriam continued: "Too, in spite of the precautions we took, I was always worried about getting pregnant. This isn't beautiful."

"I told you to take pills."

"Go to a doctor as an unmarried girl and ask for a prescription? I'm not that modern."

"I offered to withdraw early, but you didn't like it."

"I asked you to buy condoms, but you were embarrassed to ask for them in a drugstore."

"Yes, because it's usually ladies who work in drugstores and wait on you. Besides, condoms are used mostly with prostitutes and I don't consider you a prostitute, Miriam."

"I'm not blaming you, Timothy," Miriam said with all the tenderness she could put in her voice as she grasped his hand more firmly. "I'm just trying to say it wasn't so very beautiful."

"But why didn't you ever tell me that?"

"I thought you needed it and that you would be disappointed and start to doubt whether I love you."

Timothy sighed again. They were silent for a few moments.

I hadn't interrupted them on purpose. I was glad that they had started to talk frankly to each other and to share honestly their feelings. So I said:

"Why don't you go now and continue to talk, but alone, just between yourselves. I believe you have to come to your own decision. But it might well be that these more or less frustrating experiences have something to do with the uncertainty you feel about your love."

"How can we know whether we love each other?" they both asked with one voice.

The telephone rang and the operator announced Maurice.

"I'm going to answer this question tonight in my lecture," I promised.

Timothy and Miriam had just left when Maurice walked into my room. Again I was struck by his appearance. He walked in the same way that he spoke—decisively and yet without trying to make an impression. When I spoke with him, I was aware of his intelligence, yet he never tried to be brilliant. Still there was a certain contradiction in his personality. On the one hand were the manly gestures, and on the other hand, a certain helpless air; his grown-up way of expressing himself, accompanied by a boyish smile.

"Where did you leave your mother?"

"She's waiting in the car. I told her I wanted to ask you a question. She said she could not understand our conversation anyway. You remember my question: 'How does one approach a girl?' "

"Maurice, is that so difficult? Just be what you are. Don't try to make yourself interesting. Don't pretend to be someone you're not, but show that you are interested in her. Ask her about her hobbies, her likes and dislikes, her favorite books or subjects of study, her family. Try to find some common interest and then talk about that."

"As if that would be so easy."

"Tell me, Maurice, you're thirty-four years old. Didn't you ever have a girl?"

"Yes, I did, and I wanted to marry her."

"Why didn't you?"

"I sent her to the doctor for a medical checkup. He found out that she wasn't a virgin."

"And you left her for this reason?"

"Yes."

"What became of her?"

"I don't know. Do you think I did wrong?"

"Maurice, the night before yesterday you showed me the 'red-light district.' What if your girl is living now among those prostitutes? You may have pushed her into the very same fate from which you tried to save your mother."

Maurice said nothing.

"What makes me so mad is that double moral standard: Girls must remain virgins. Men must have sex. It's so illogical, so unjust."

"But don't you think one must have some experience before marriage? You can't enter marriage completely inexperienced."

"Everyone enters marriage inexperienced, Maurice. You see, each person is different and therefore each couple is doubly different. Consequently, these premarital experiences become a burden rather than a help for your marriage. The choice is only between two things: either you enter into marriage with no experience or with the wrong kind of experience.—But excuse me, I think we have to leave now. The lecture begins at six-thirty."

As we were walking down the stairs, Maurice asked:

"Why do you think it is so hard to convince young people that by experimenting before marriage, they have the wrong kind of experience?"

"Because they can know this only after they have had the right kind."

"So you don't think it's because of a strong sex drive?"

"I don't think it's primarily a sexual problem at all. They need someone whom they can trust to such an extent that they will believe he or she is telling the truth, even if they are not yet able to experience it. They need to accept a truth which they cannot yet prove by way of experimentation. Only when they have this degree of confidence can they be sure that they are not being cheated, but rather helped toward a rewarding goal."

We reached the car. Maurice's mother greeted me with great friendliness and politeness.

"Ask her what she thinks about the triangle," I said to Maurice as we were driving to the church.

Shilah, Maurice's mother, made a long speech. He smiled as she spoke and then summed it up for me:

"She doesn't think of a triangle at all. She thinks of a three-legged stool. Such a stool can never wobble so long as it has three legs, even though the legs are of different length or the ground is uneven. But if you take one leg off, then you'll fall to the ground."

"You have a remarkable mother, Maurice. Tell her I like her comparison very much and ask her whether she could think of polygamy also as a three-legged stool."

He translated and she answered.

"She says that a polygamous marriage always wobbles. It makes you fall to the ground. She would never have become the second wife of a married man—rather she would die."

6

AS WE APPROACHED the church, we saw people coming from that direction.

"The church is full," Maurice commented. "Those who didn't find a place are leaving already."

He was right. Not only were the pews crowded, but people were standing in the aisles. We had difficulty getting through. Chairs were placed even in the front of the church, around the altar. Some elderly, very dignified men were seated there.

Again fear gripped my heart. I knew some of the problems now. But by far not all of them. It was impossible to judge how my words would affect their lives, cut into them, cause hope or despair. It was an overwhelming responsibility.

One of the older men led in prayer. This comforted me. He wouldn't have done that, I thought, had the older people been offended.

When Daniel took his place beside me in the pulpit, I felt strengthened. I became calm, reminding myself that it was not my message I had come to deliver but God's.

The first person I spotted in the audience was Fatma. She was seated in one of the back pews on the women's side. Her face, with the bright and hungry eyes, stood out from all the others. "Please give me a word for her," I prayed silently.

There were quite a few newcomers who had not been in church the two previous evenings. So I decided to sum up briefly what I had said before:

"There are three things which belong essentially to a marriage: to leave one's parents, to cleave to each other, and to become one flesh. In other words, there is a legal, a personal, and a physical aspect of marriage. They are inseparable. If you do separate them, the whole thing falls apart.

"One of you just told me that marriage is like a three-legged stool. If one of the legs is lacking, the stool won't hold you up when you sit on it."

I saw faces brighten up. This was a good image. Shilah was right.

"Last night we discussed the question: Should we approach marriage first from the legal, the personal, or the physical side? What is the best way?

"We talked about two answers to this question, the traditional answer and the modern answer. The traditional answer was to start with the legal aspect, with the wedding. Here the great danger is that the personal aspect, the aspect of love, is then left out of the picture. This is why young people in your midst rebel today against this traditional answer, for they are just in the process of discovering the beauty of this personal aspect.

"The modern answer was to start with the physical aspect, with sex. The danger is that then the legal aspect is left out and it never comes to a wedding. This is why the older people among you rebel against this modern answer. They are afraid that family life will deteriorate altogether.

"Today we shall hear the biblical answer to our question. In order to find this answer we have to consider the first word of our key Bible verse, Genesis 2:24:

Therefore

"'*Therefore* a man leaves his father and his mother and cleaves to his wife, and they become one flesh.'

"In order to understand this word 'therefore' we must recall the story which comes before it. It is a well-known and often ridiculed story. It tells about the incomprehensible kindness of God which He wanted to show to man when He made him a 'helpmeet,' a 'helper fit for him,' a partner equal to him, completing him:

" 'So the Lord God caused a deep sleep to fall upon the man, and while he slept took one of his ribs and closed up its place with flesh; and the rib which the Lord God had taken from the man he made into a woman and brought her to the man.'

"This story is the most wonderful and unique description of the reality of love.

"Why do the two sexes long for each other without ceasing? How can it be explained that they are magnetically attracted to each other? The answer is: They are made out of the same piece—just like the Liberian carving I showed you the other night. They are parts of a whole and want to restore this whole again, want to complete each other, want to become 'one flesh.'

"The power which drives them toward each other is the power of love.

"*Therefore,* truly, for love's sake, the two shall leave their parents, cleave to each other and become one.

The Love Entrance

"When we ask ourselves the question, at which angle do we enter the marriage triangle, the Bible would answer, at the angle of cleaving."

I took my wooden triangle in my hand and pointed to the left angle: "It is this angle of cleaving which is the best door to use to enter the triangle. Love has to precede marriage and sex. It is not marriage which leads to love, but love which leads to marriage. It is not sex which creates love, but love which seeks, among other things, also the physical expression.

"The entrance at the angle of love is the most promising as far as the development and unfolding of the dynamism of the triangle is concerned. Therefore it corresponds with God's will.

"There is another reason why God wants us to enter through the door of love. The public and legal act of the wedding as well as the sex act create irrevocable facts, while love does not.

"An engaged couple may one day feel that they made a decision too soon, that the time was not yet ripe and that their engagement was a mistake. They then have the possibility of breaking their engagement without causing an incurable wound to the partner. For love's sake they can let each other go."

At this point I could not help but think of Miriam and Timothy and look for their faces in the audience. I spotted them sitting together in the very last pew. Miriam was the only girl sitting on the men's side of the church. After all, I thought, they can shun their traditions if they want to.

"So long as the other two angles are not involved, the angle of love is like a revolving door—a door through which you can enter, but in case of necessity, through which you can also leave.

"The wedding act is not like a revolving door. It's like a door which shuts and there is no handle inside. Of course, it can be forced open. But this is much more difficult. We could say that a divorce is more difficult and has more consequences than a broken engagement, regrettable as this may be.

"The same is true about the sex act. It also creates an irrevocable fact.

"According to biblical thinking, two human beings who have shared the sexual act are never the same afterward. They can no longer act toward each other as if they had not had this experience. It makes out of those involved in it a couple bound to each other. It creates a one-flesh bond with all its implications.

"According to the Bible, this is the case regardless of whether the couple is serious or not, regardless of whether they intend to get married or not; yes, says the Apostle Paul, it is true even in the case of prostitution. In I Corinthians 6:16 we read: 'Do you not know that he who joins himself to a prostitute becomes one body with her?'

"After the sex act they are a couple in spite of themselves.

"Robert Grimm says: 'The flesh has an indelible stamp imprinted upon it. I cannot divorce myself from my own body.' "*

There was a movement at the back of the church. Someone wanted to leave, but since the door was blocked by late-comers, this created quite a disturbance.

I recognized the person who left. It was Fatma.

From then on, I was ill at ease. I told myself maybe it was because

* See Robert Grimm, *Love and Sexuality* (London: Hodder & Stoughton; U.S. edition, New York: Association Press), pp. 52, 56, 66.

we had started late and she had to be back at school before John came to pick her up. But somehow this explanation didn't satisfy me. I had the feeling that something was wrong. For the moment, though, I had no choice. I must continue:

"I repeat: You may also succeed if you enter through one of the other doors, but it is risky. If you want to retreat, you will hurt your partner and yourself.

"This leads us to a very practical question. I know many young couples who say: 'We would like to enter through the door of love. But how can we know that our love is deep enough to lead us to a life-long cleaving, to complete faithfulness? How can we be sure that our love is mature enough to take the wedding vows and promise to stay together all our lives until death separates us? If sex is no test of love, what is the test then?'

"May I give you my answer:

Six Tests of Love*

First: **The sharing test** "Real love wants to share, to give, to reach out. It thinks of the other one, not of himself. When you read something, how often do you have the thought, I would like to share this with my friend? When you plan something, do you think of what you would like to do or what the other one would enjoy?

"As Hermann Oeser, a German author, has put it: 'Those who want to become happy should not marry. The important thing is to make the other one happy.—Those who want to be understood should not marry. The important thing is to understand one's partner.'

"The first test question then is this: Are we able to share together? Do I want to become happy or make happy?

Second: **The strength test** "I got a letter once from a worried lover. He had read somewhere that one loses weight if one is truly in love. In spite of all his feelings of love, he didn't lose weight and that worried him.

"It is true that the love experience can also affect you physically. But in the long run, real love should not take away your strength;

* Some of these tests I have taken from the fine book written by Evelyn Duvall, *Love and the Facts of Life* (New York: Association Press, 1963).

instead, it should give you new energy and strength. It should fill you with joy and make you creative, willing to accomplish even more.

"Second test question: Does our love give us new strength and fill us with creative energy, or does it take away our strength and energy?

Third: The respect test "There is no real love without respect, without being able to look up to the other one.

"A girl may admire a boy when she watches him play soccer and score all the goals. But if she asks herself the question: 'Do I want this boy to be the father of my children?' very often the answer will be in the negative.

"A boy may admire a girl when he sees her dancing. But if he asks himself the question: 'Do I want this girl to be the mother of my children?' she may look very different to him.

"Third test question: Do we really have enough respect for each other? Am I proud of my partner?

Fourth: The habit test "Once a European girl who was engaged came to me and was very worried: 'I love my fiancé very much,' she said, 'but I just can't stand the way he eats an apple.'"

There was understanding laughter in the audience.

"Love accepts the other one *with* his habits. Don't marry on the installment plan, thinking that these things will change later on. Very likely they will not. You must accept the other one as he is now, including his habits and shortcomings.

"Fourth test question: Do we only love each other or do we also like each other?

Fifth test: The quarrel test "When a couple come to me and want to get married, I always ask them if they have once had a real quarrel —not just a casual difference of opinion, but a real fight.

"Many times they will say: 'Oh, no! Pastor, we love each other.'

"Then I tell them: 'Quarrel first—and then I will marry you.'

"The point is, of course, not the quarreling, but the ability to be reconciled to each other. This ability must be trained and tested before marriage. Not sex, but rather this quarrel test, is a 'required' premarital experience.

"Fifth test question: Are we able to forgive each other and to give in to each other?

Sixth: The time test "A young couple came to me to be married.

'How long have you known each other?' I asked. 'Already three, almost four weeks,' was the answer.

"This is too short. One year, I would say, is the minimum. Two years may be safer. It is good to see each other, not only on holidays and in Sunday clothes, but also at work, in daily living, unshaved and in a T-shirt, or with hair that needs to be washed and set, in situations of stress or danger.

"There is an old saying: 'Never get married until you have summered and wintered with your partner.'

"In case you are in doubt about your feeling of love, time will tell.

"Last test question: Has our love summered and wintered? Do we know each other long enough?

"And may I make a final statement with all clarity: Sex is no test of love."

Here I was interrupted. Daniel told me many people asked if I would write down the six tests on the blackboard. I agreed. I wrote in English on the left side—Daniel wrote on the right.

It took quite a long time. Many took notes. Daniel discovered to his dismay that some who had no paper along used the pages of the hymnbook to take down the tests of love.

Then I wrote under the six tests with large capital letters:

SEX IS NO TEST OF LOVE

I don't know how Daniel translated it, but I thought, We have made some progress since the day before yesterday in that we could write the word "sex" on a blackboard placed in front of the altar!

I explained:

"If a couple want to use the sex act in order to know whether they love each other, one has to ask them: 'Do you love each other so little?' If both of them think: 'Tonight we must have sex—otherwise my partner will think that I don't love him or that he does not love me,' the fear of a possible failure is sufficient to prevent the success of the experiment.

"Sex is no test of love, for it is precisely the very thing that one wants to test which is destroyed by the testing.

"Try to observe yourself when you go to sleep. Either you observe yourself, then you don't fall asleep. Or you fall asleep, and then you haven't observed yourself.

"The same is true about sex as a test of love. Either you test, then you don't love. Or you love, then you don't test.

"For its own sake, love needs to wait with its physical expression until it can be included in the dynamism of the triangle.

"This waiting is usually harder for the young man than for the girl. Therefore, the girl has to help the young man here, who, because of his natural impetuousness, is more tempted to aim short of the goal.

"The first help she can give him is to learn how to say 'no' without wounding, how to refuse without breaking off. This is an art. She will soon discover, however, that a simple and definite 'no' is more helpful and effective than long explanations and excuses. If he loves her, the young man will respect her the more because of it. She will have to teach him, too, that an honest compliment may be more meaningful to her than a passionate embrace.

"Another help she can give him is through her ability to blush. One says that formerly girls blushed when they were embarrassed. Today they are embarrassed when they blush. But this blushing, this natural reaction of shame, is nothing to be ashamed of. It is a defense and a protection at the same time. Girls should consider their natural feeling of shame and modesty in certain situations as a gift and put it into the service of love."

It was now completely quiet in the church. I knew that this natural feeling of shame and modesty is still much more prevalent in African society than in Western society. Scenes in movies showing long and elaborate kissing are repugnant to Africans. The audience gets restless when they appear on the screen and some refuse to look at them. Still these movies are shown all over Africa and those who see them start to distrust their own feelings. This is why I owed them a word of reassurance.

Daniel and I were still standing in front of the first pews. I checked with him on the time. He said I could go on for another ten or fifteen minutes. So I decided to close by dealing with the special situation of engaged couples:

"Let's imagine now that we have a couple who did not enter into the triangle through the sex entrance, but through the love entrance. Their situation is different and we have to discern very carefully these two approaches.

"They have known each other for a long time. They do not need to test their love by sex. They have learned how to share. They both have more energy and strength because of their love. Their mutual respect has deepened. They have accepted the habits of each other and really like each other. They have quarreled and gone through stormy times. They know they can forgive each other.

"They are now at the point where they can make the promise to each other: 'We want to cleave together for life.' This means they become engaged. They have entered the triangle through the door of love— love resolved to cleave. But now they have to make a crucial decision: 'Which of the two other angles shall we reach first? Shall we first get married and then sleep together or first sleep together and then get married?' "

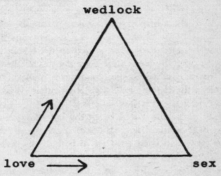

I paused, looked at the young people, and said: "What do you think?"

It was as if I had pulled a cork out of a bottle. Everyone started to talk at once. After some effort Daniel was able to quiet them down. I repeated:

"This situation is entirely different from the one we had yesterday when we discussed the 'sex entrance.' This couple do not consider sex as the first step without any commitment to each other. They have committed themselves and this after a long and careful examination. They really have no egoistical motives but have accepted responsibility for each other.

"Now they ask: 'Why can't we express this love also in a physical way? Why must we first get an official license to go to bed together? Is it really that piece of paper which brings marriage into being?'

"Of course it isn't—any more than a birth certificate brings a baby into being. Still, it's more than just a piece of paper. It protects human life legally.

"The same is true about the marriage license. It protects marriage legally. We have seen that the legal aspect is as essential for the unfolding of the play of forces within the marriage triangle as is the personal and the physical aspect.

"Those engaged couples who want to take a right turn and start their marriage before the wedding overlook one fact: the unpredictability of human life. How can they be so sure that they will get married?

"What if one of them dies before the wedding? Car accident? Heart attack? Is he then a widower or not? Is she a widow? Can they inherit from each other? Is she a Miss or a Mrs.? And in case she is pregnant— what is the family name of the child? These questions show that a marriage license is more than a piece of paper. So long as they are not yet ready to take the legal step, they are not ready to take full responsibility for each other. Responsibility calls for legality.

"Does this mean they suppress all signs of affection? Walk first to the altar and then expect the great revelation?

"No, certainly not. This would block the unfolding of the play of forces just as much as the disregard of the legal aspect. The secret is that the lovers grow and make progress in both directions at the same time without skipping any of the steps."

I turned to the blackboard and drew parallel lines in this way:

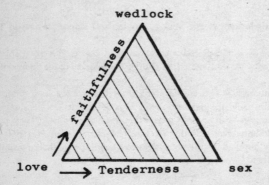

"Each step in the direction of faithfulness and wedlock should go hand in hand with the deepening of tenderness and intimacy, until finally, coming from the entrance of love, the two other angles—wedlock and sexual union—are reached at the same time.

"Only from the perspective of the goal can this question be answered. The point is that each step toward intimacy must be balanced by the same measure of responsibility and faithfulness."

I turned to Daniel, who stood beside me, and asked him in a voice that all could hear:

"How about your young people? Do they usually reach the two angles at the same time?"

There was loud laughter even among the older people. Daniel smiled knowingly and waited until it was quiet again. Then he became serious. I sat down in the first bench beside Maurice, who whispered in my ear the interpretation of what Daniel was saying:

"What usually happens here is this: The young man says to the girl, 'I love you,' and what he means is just an inch in the direction of faithfulness. But the girl is so happy about it that she, in turn, allows him to go three inches in the direction of intimacy."

Again an outburst of laughter.

"Then the boy thinks, This worked fine, so he adds another inch toward faithfulness. The girl replies by giving him four more inches in the direction of intimacy. Before they know it, they end up at the sex angle, without being able to carry the full responsibility for this step. Instead of parallel lines you then have slanted lines."

Then Daniel rubbed out my parallel lines and replaced them with slanting lines:

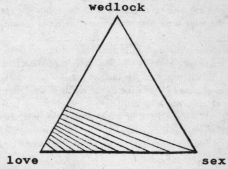

I marveled at Daniel's way of illustrating the situation so simply. He motioned to me, and I again took my place at his side to finish the lecture.

"As you see," I said, pointing to the slanting lines of the triangle, "there is now a vacuum, an empty space in the triangle. This is the situation of many of our engaged couples in America and Europe, too. They think they love each other. But then they go too far too soon. An emptiness creeps into their relationship. They become less and less sure of their love. So they intensify their intimacies in the hope of intensifying their love. The more they do it, the less they are sure of their love.

"On the other hand, they don't dare to break their engagement because they have already gone too far. So they get married, but they carry this emptiness into their marriage and thereby lay the foundation for many troubles and problems later on.

"To keep the parallel lines from slanting is a difficult job. It takes more than human wisdom and strength. It needs divine wisdom and strength. It needs the help of the master artist of marriage who is God Himself.

"He knows why He relates the three elements of marriage—leaving, cleaving, one flesh—so closely together that they become inseparable. We have to trust Him and know that by doing so He does not want to take something away from us, but He wants to give us something—to help us create a work of art. This confidence and trust in Him will give us strength to obey His divine will:

" 'Therefore a man leaves his father and his mother and cleaves to his wife, and they become one flesh.'

"In closing, let me call your attention to the following verse: 'And the man and the wife were both naked, and were not ashamed' (Gen. 2:25).

"This verse has a strange place in the Bible. It hovers between paradise and the fallen world. It is the final phrase of the creation story, just before the fall is reported. In this way it is a hint that marriage reflects a feeble glimmer of paradise in the midst of the fallen world.

" 'Naked, and . . . not ashamed.'

" 'Naked' is not meant here in a physical sense only. It means to stand in front of each other, stripped and undisguised, without pretension, without hiding anything, seeing the partner as he or she really is and showing myself to him or her as I really am—and still not to be ashamed.

"'Naked, and . . . not ashamed.'

"But this ultimate goal of mature love is promised only to those who, as the previous verse says, have left father and mother and cleave to each other; in other words, those who have been publicly and legally married.

"These two—not the ones before or outside of marriage—become one flesh. It is very meaningful that the Bible uses the term 'becoming one flesh' only in the context of marriage.

"These two—not the ones before or outside of marriage—shall succeed in the tremendously difficult task of facing each other as they really are, of living with each other—naked and yet not ashamed.

"Maybe there has to be a sense of shame before marriage in order for there to be within marriage the grace of not being ashamed.

"'Naked, and . . . not ashamed.' This is what the Bible means by the word 'to know.' 'Adam knew Eve his wife' (Gen. 4:1).

"Husband and wife can 'know' each other only within the tent.

"'Therefore a man leaves his father and his mother and cleaves to his wife, and they become one flesh.'"

7

AS SOON as I had finished, I hurried to the door. My heart was not at rest because of Fatma. I didn't even wait for the closing hymn. The last thing I heard was Daniel announcing something in the native language. I took it that he was saying there would be no meeting on Saturday night, but that I would preach on Sunday and it was hoped that my wife could be present at that time too.

I asked some of the young people, who I knew understood English, about Fatma. They could tell me only that they had seen her leave hurriedly.

My apprehension grew.

"Did someone accompany her?"

"No, she left alone."

Maurice took me home in his car, but by a different route.

"Where are you going?" I asked.

"I'm taking my mother home first. Then I would like to invite you to have your evening meal with me in our finest restaurant."

"Wouldn't your mother like to come with us?"

"Oh, no, she wouldn't feel at ease in a restaurant. She belongs to the generation that prefers the 'three-legged stool.'"

Shilah was tired and didn't talk. We let her off at her home and returned to the city, where Maurice stopped in front of a very modern building.

As soon as we were seated and had given our orders, Maurice began shooting questions at me:

"Did you know you contradicted yourself tonight?"

"Did I?"

"Yes, first you said that according to the Apostle Paul the sex act creates a one-flesh bond even if one has intercourse with a prostitute. Then you said the Bible uses the term 'one flesh' only in context with marriage."

Maurice had a triumphant grin.

"You are right," I said. "I Corinthians 6:16 is indeed, according to the Greek text, the only place where this expression is not used in context with marriage. But I think this is in order to demonstrate the absurdity of becoming one flesh outside of marriage. It is absurd to become one flesh with a prostitute. Paul wants to say: 'Outside of marriage, this act is entirely out of context.'"

Maurice thought for awhile as the soup was being served. Then he said:

"Yes, but are they now one flesh or are they not one flesh? You see, first you said that they became one flesh through the sexual union, even if they were not serious or did not intend to marry, in other words, without even wanting to build a tent—and then you said that they can fully become one flesh only within the tent, within marriage."

"Oh, Maurice. You are too intelligent for me. You put your finger exactly on the weakest point of my lecture."

"If a man can become one flesh with a prostitute, then everyone who sleeps just once with a prostitute would be married to her."

"I said, the act forms the couple. I didn't say they are married."

"And what's the difference?"

"That's precisely the question."

Maurice looked puzzled. We were silent for several moments.

"You see, Maurice, what you touch on here is indeed an unanswered question. But there are two things which are clear to me. First: the sexual union is a very consequential action even if it involves a prostitute. Second: to become one flesh involves much more than just the sexual union even with your own wife. We have to grope for the right way somewhere between these two truths."

Maurice sighed. Two truths—it's much easier to have everything straight, right down the line.

"So they are an unwed couple," Maurice suggested.

"Put it the other way around: they are coupled unweds. That way it sounds more absurd."

"Where would prostitution fit into your triangle?"

"It is the complete isolation of the right angle. Sex alone, separate from love and marriage."

"And yet they enter the tent? Become one?"

"How can I describe this absurdity with an image? It is as if they enter the tent and then discover that it has no top. They open the door to a house, lock it behind them, and then see that it has neither walls nor a roof. They go in and still they end up being outside."

We were interrupted as the waiter brought the next course. After he left Maurice said:

"You stung my conscience this afternoon when you blamed me for not marrying that girl who was no longer a virgin. Would you say that as a general rule, one could marry nonvirgins, without qualifying this statement?"

"No, of course not. It all depends upon the girl, her character, the circumstances under which it happened, her attitude toward this fact. But when I see these girls, many of them thirteen, fourteen years old, I can't help but feel sorry for them. No one has given them any sex education. The only thing they were taught is that because they are girls, they must obey all men. Then a man came and they obeyed. They were not trained to resist . . . You see, Maurice, virginity is not just a mark of the body, a question of having the hymen or not. To me it is much more a question of the heart, of the ability to love. It is not something which a girl loses, but which she gives."

"I don't follow you."

"Every girl has a unique gift—the ability to give herself completely once to a man. This gift is like capital in the bank. But many girls spend it in small coins. Every day they draw a little bit out of their capital, and in flirtations, here and there, throw it to the wind. Technically speaking, such a girl may still be a virgin, but she has lost her ability to love through a lot of necking and petting experiences. On the other hand, there may be a girl of whom some man took advantage because she was inexperienced. Technically speaking, she lost her virginity, but as far as her heart is concerned, I would call her a virgin."

"I would like to tell you something," Maurice replied. He paused. "Whether you believe it or not, Walter, I am still inexperienced. I am still a virgin."

"Thank you for telling me, Maurice. I believe you."

Then he asked: "Do you understand now, Walter, why it was especially hard for me to think of marrying a girl who was not a virgin?"

"No."

"Even as a Christian?"

"Just because you are a Christian. Who else could do it, if not a Christian? I don't see otherwise how you could pray honestly the Lord's Prayer: 'Forgive us our trespasses, as we forgive those who trespass against us.' "

"But forgiveness must be mutual."

"She goofed in this respect. You goofed in others. What's the difference? I can't think of any better glue for cleaving to each other than mutual forgiveness. Just that is the uniqueness of life with God. He is always ready to begin anew with us. Therefore, we can always begin anew with others. And I tell you, there is not a single day in marriage when you don't have to begin anew in some respect with your wife. And she with you."

We finished our meal in silence. But this silence was part of our conversation, not the end of it. On the way back to the hotel I asked Maurice whether he would consider marrying a widow.

I couldn't have asked him anything more alien to his thinking. Had his hands not been on the steering wheel, he probably would have thrown them up in the air.

"What makes you say that?"

"I feel a strong sympathy for young widows in Africa. No one takes care of them. They have no pension, no social security. They are not all prostitutes. Some try to make an honest living. I wish they could have a husband like you. Take a young widow with children. You would make a good father at your age. I can just see your mother's face if you would bring five grandchildren home to her at one time!"

Maurice had to take a deep breath.

"You must be joking," he said.

"No," I assured him, "I'm not."

"You really think that a widow of approximately my age could be a better partner for me than a young girl?"

"She could be a partner, not a daughter."

"And if I had my own children with her, wouldn't that be difficult?"

"Yes, but it would be much less difficult than bringing up children without a father, and for the children, much less difficult than having a mother who could be the daughter of their father."

"Then I could marry a divorcee too?"

"Depending upon the circumstances, yes. Either we believe in forgiveness or we don't."

We reached the hotel and entered the lobby. I asked the clerk for my key.

"Walter," Maurice said, "you turn everything upside down in me."

"I don't want you to become an old maid."

Maurice laughed and gave me a spontaneous hug.

The clerk, who had overheard our last words, looked at us in amazement. "There was a gentleman calling for you several times," he said.

"Did he leave his number for me to call back?"

"No, sir. He said he would call again."

At this moment, the operator came out of her booth and said that the man was calling again.

"Put it through, please. I will take it in my room."

I hurriedly said good-night to Maurice. As I was waiting for the elevator, he returned and gave me his card. "In case you need me, you can call me any time. I am free tomorrow."

I picked up the telephone as soon as I got to my room.

"This is John."

"I'm very glad you called me. How are you? Have you thought over our talk last night?"

"Sir, I want to tell you something," he said in a cold, harsh voice. "The dirt on my hands is honest dirt. It got there through hard work. I am proud of it. My work is harder than chatting with girls in hotels. And the way I dress is my business, not yours. Also, Fatma is my business. I know how to take care of her. I told you that story about leaving the country in order to see your reactions. I know what I want to do. You can't interfere in my affairs. And if you don't send Fatma home immediatley, I will call the police."

"She is not here."

"I don't believe you."

"I assure you, she is not here."

"I don't believe one word of what you say. She wasn't in the house when I came home from work. She sneaked out through the window. I know that she went to church."

"Please listen, John. I'm very sorry that I hurt you. I apologize for that remark about your hands. But the important thing now is to find Fatma."

"I know she went to church."

"Yes, she was in church. But she left early. I thought she probably had to meet you."

"It's now eleven o'clock. If she's not home by midnight, I'm going to call the police and accuse you if something has happened to her."

"Please tell me, John . . ."

But he had hung up. I tried to breathe calmly. I had made a horrible mistake. The remarks about his hands had been unnecessary. Every negative remark about someone is a prayer to the devil, I thought, and is fulfilled immediately.

How did he know about it, though? Was it possible that Fatma had told him? But he had said he didn't see her all day. Or had he lied to me?

And where was Fatma? It is dangerous for a girl to go out alone at night. Anything could have happened to her. If only I had the slightest idea where she lived! Where could she have gone?

I went to bed with a feeling of helplessness and powerlessness. If I had had the slightest idea where to search for her, I would not have hesitated to go out again. Indeed I wondered what counselors who are unable to pray would do in such a situation.

I don't know how long I had been asleep when I suddenly woke. It was as if I had heard a voice in my room. John's voice. Then I remembered I had dreamed of him, reliving his visit in my dream: he was about to leave and I asked him whether he had far to go. "No, just across the river," he had said. It was now close to 3:00 a.m.

An anxious thought flashed through my mind.

I went to the telephone and picked up the receiver. A sleepy voice answered. It was the night clerk.

"Tell me, is there a river in this city?"

"Yes, sir."

"A big one?"

"A little bit big."

"How far is it from here?"

"It's a little bit far."

"How long does it take to walk there?"

"A little bit long."

This could mean anything between fifteen minutes and two hours.

"I didn't see any river when I went to the church where I lectured."

"That's because you don't have to cross the bridge to get there."

"Tell me, if someone is here at the hotel and says, 'I live just across the river,' does he have to go over that bridge?"

"Yes, sir."

"And when he goes from Christ Church and wants to get on the other side of the river, does he have to cross the same bridge?"

"Yes, sir."

"Is there only one bridge?"

"There is only one bridge, sir."

"Are there taxis available now?"

"It is difficult. I wouldn't suggest that you take a taxi alone now."

"Then please dial this number."

I heard the ringing sound for a long time. Then Maurice answered.

"This is Walter, Maurice. You told me I could call you any time. I need you right now."

"I'm at your disposition."

"How long does it take for you to get to the hotel?"

"Fifteen minutes."

"Try to make it in ten."

I got dressed, went down and waited for Maurice in front of the hotel. The streets were entirely empty of people and traffic. Finally, the light of Maurice's car appeared. He stopped and I climbed in.

"Do you know where the bridge is?"

He laughed.

"Please don't ask me any questions. Just take me to the bridge, but before you drive onto the bridge, pull over to the side and stop."

We drove silently. I was glad Maurice didn't ask any questions. Then I saw the bridge. It was long and narrow with a stone balustrade on either side. There was a small walk for pedestrians on the right side.

Maurice stopped as we approached, but in a spot where we could see out over the whole bridge. There were no street lights, but there was moonlight and we could easily see the other side.

There she was. There was Fatma, leaning over the balustrade and staring down at the rushing waters.

"Do you see that girl there?"

"Yes.".

"I can't tell you her story now. But I know she is desperate and might commit suicide. Is there a police station close by?"

"There is one on the other side of the bridge."

"All right. Drive now onto the bridge. Go past her about twenty feet, so that she'll think we're driving on. Then stop and I will jump out and try to catch her before she jumps."

"And if she jumps?"

"Then go as fast as you can to the police and give the alarm."

"Okay."

"If you see me talking to her quietly, then turn around and park a little distance away, so that you can't hear us, but you must see us."

"Why?"

"There may be a lawsuit. I need a witness for everything I do with this girl. Let's go now."

"Shall we have a word of prayer?"

"Please."

There was no time to lose. Maurice prayed for a few moments, his folded hands resting on the wheel. I looked at those faithful hands and knew they were more than human hands.

Fatma didn't move as we approached her. She remained standing with her back turned toward us, leaning on her elbows, her eyes fixed on the water.

Maurice passed her slowly, then stopped. I threw open the door, jumped out and ran toward her as fast as I could. She whirled around, frightened. Before she had a chance to react further, I grabbed her by the arm.

"Fatma, foolish girl, what are you doing?" I cried.

She looked at me for a second, then, struggling free, turned to resume her position. She didn't say a word as she continued to stare at the moving water.

Maurice drove on a short distance, turned around, and parked on the other side, about a hundred yards away. He turned off the headlights. There was no one else on the bridge, just the three of us.

The quietness was interrupted only by the sound of the gurgling water below us.

I stood beside Fatma, leaning with my elbows on the stone balustrade and looking down into the water just as she was doing.

After a short pause, I asked her in a voice as calm and relaxed as possible: "Do you know where you will get when you jump down there?"

She did not reply and I waited. Minutes passed.

"I don't care," she said finally. "The main thing is that it is finished."

"It isn't finished. That's precisely where you make the mistake."

"When I am dead, it will be finished."

"You will not be dead and it won't be finished."

"But the burden will be gone."

"On the contrary. You will take your burdens along with you into eternity. And the burden of having committed suicide in addition to all the others. It solves nothing, absolutely nothing."

"What does it matter? All I know is I can't go on living like this. I can't carry the burden any longer."

"I didn't ask you to. I want you to live without the burden."

"Pastor, you don't know what you are saying. You don't even know half of my burden. I lied to you. I lied to everybody. It's much worse than you think. You would be shocked if you knew the truth about me, the whole truth."

"I promise you, I shall not be shocked."

Without moving, she looked down at the dark water. Then she said:

"If I don't take my own life, I might take someone else's. Death is what I deserve."

"I agree."

"You agree?"

"Yes, whether I know everything about you or not—you deserve death. So do I. Everybody does. The only difference is that some know it and some don't. I'm glad you do."

"Why don't you let me die, then?"

"Because you are too late. Someone else has already died your death."

"It's too late to change my life, but not yet too late to die."

"The other way around, Fatma: It's not yet too late to change your life, but much too late to die."

"Too late to die?" She turned her head and looked at me. "I don't understand."

"Let me tell you a story. Have you ever heard of Barabbas?"

"You mean the murderer who was a fellow prisoner of Jesus?"

"Yes, that's the one. It was the Jewish custom to release a prisoner at the time of the Passover. Pilate asked the Jews whom he should release—Jesus or Barabbas."

"I remember, and they chose Barabbas."

"Right! Now just imagine—Barabbas was free and was walking through the streets of Jerusalem on that Good Friday. He saw the crowds of people streaming out to Golgotha and followed them. When he arrived there, whom did he see?"

"Jesus on the cross."

"You learned your lesson well at that village school."

"I heard the story often, but it never meant anything to me."

"Now listen, Barabbas recognized his fellow prisoner. Suddenly it dawned on him: If Jesus were not hanging there . . . Can you finish the sentence, Fatma?"

"Then I would be in his place," she said.

"Yes, Fatma, you would. And I would. Both of us would."

We were silent again and watched the water swirling by.

"Continue the story," she said after awhile, again without looking at me.

"Imagine Barabbas would have thought, it's unjust that He dies. After all, I am the murderer, not He. I have deserved death, not He. All I can do now is to kill myself. What would you think about that?"

"He would have been foolish."

"Exactly, just as foolish as you would be if you jumped down there. You are too late, Fatma. The death you have deserved Jesus has already died. Since his death, every suicide is too late. It's unnecessary. You are free. Free like Barabbas."

"Free?" She turned around and looked me fully in the face, leaning with her back toward the balustrade. The apathy was gone. In her eyes was desperation. "Free? I am free?" A short, bitter laugh. "I am locked in, Pastor. The door fell shut behind me. The door without a handle."

"Is that why you left the church so early?"

"Yes, you took away from me the last straw of hope."

I shut my eyes. What had I done? What kind of a messenger had I been?

"I entered the tent. And when I was inside, I found it had no top. It was raining in. But still I couldn't get out. Then I had this horrible feeling of being locked in. I wanted to get out. Any place. To jump! Any place!"

I stood in front of her with my eyes shut. I shuddered. "Fatma, I . . ."

"What does it matter whether I am married or not? 'Afterward they are a couple,' you said, 'in spite of themselves.' I am coupled in spite of myself."

She started to shout, forgetting herself in wrath and desperation.

"I am marked. The flesh has an indelible imprint upon it, you said. I am marked, marked, marked. Not just with John. With at least six others before. My door is six times shut, Pastor. Or maybe six doors and no one to break the locks.

"One flesh, yes, one flesh," Fatma continued. "But not with everything 'I am and I have' but just with this poor, dirty, damned body. 'You can't divorce yourself from your own body,' you said. All right, I can't. I am not married and still I'm not divorceable."

The law kills, I thought. The law kills. If she would have jumped from that bridge, it would have been my fault, not John's. You, Who woke me up tonight, give me the right word now. On this bridge between heaven and earth, between two banks of a river, between death and life, give me Your word.

"Fatma, the church was full of young people. They had not yet built their tents. I had to warn them, to save them from the same fate as yours. This was not the message for you."

"And what is my message?" She had turned around again and was leaning over the balustrade.

"That God can break the door open from the outside—regardless of whether there is one, or six, or a hundred."

"Divorcing me from my own body?"

" 'With men it is impossible, but not with God; for all things are possible with God.' "

"And how could He do the impossible for me?"

"I haven't told you the end of the story yet. Barabbas realized that if Jesus were not hanging there, he would be. Barabbas didn't stop there. He turned around. With the cross behind him and the world in front of him, he said: 'Because He has died for me, I will at least live for Him.' "

Fatma said nothing. I waited. Then John 8:11 came to me for her:

"Jesus said to the adulteress: 'Neither do I condemn you; go, and do not sin again.' "

"Go where?"

"Did you read Psalm 27 as I told you on the telephone?"

"Yes, and I found my verse."

"Can you say it?"

" 'My father and my mother have forsaken me.' For me everything is turned around. It's not like you said in your lecture, not I who have left father and mother. They have forsaken me."

"I wasn't thinking of that verse for you. But if you quote it, then you must also listen to how the verse ends: 'For my father and mother have forsaken me, *but the Lord will take me up.*' "

"And where is the Lord?"

"Right now I am His mouthpiece and in His name let me tell you the verse which deeply comforted me yesterday and which I thought of as the verse for you:

> " 'For he will hide me in his shelter
>   in the day of trouble;
> he will conceal me under the cover of his tent,
>   he will set me high upon a rock.' " (Psalm 27:5)

"No," she replied, "Jeremiah is better for me: 'My tent is destroyed, and all my cords are broken; my children have gone from me, and they are not. . . .' Remember, I aborted them. I killed them. 'There is no one to spread my tent again, and to set up my curtains.' "

"But there is, Fatma. God Himself is your tent."

"You mean, I can have a tent—even living alone, single, unmarried?"

"Yes, a complete, waterproof tent, with a top and everything, a shelter where you can hide in the day of trouble."

She turned again to the balustrade, but she did not look down into the river. Her eyes followed the river to the horizon. The clear, dark African sky gave way to a tender gray—the first sign of a new day.

"I can't enter God's tent with all my sins. I forgot Him, left Him out of my life."

"He did not forget you, but He does forget your sins."

"How can you say that without knowing them?"

"I can, absolutely, even without knowing them."

"And when God forgets them?"

"It is as if they had not happened."

"I can't believe that. Not yet. Give me time to think. Help me to build my tent."

"I will."

"I can't go home now. I am afraid . . ."

"Then I suggest we go to Pastor Daniel's house first."

I gave Maurice a sign. He started up the motor of his car and drove to where we were standing. I made Fatma sit beside him and sat in the back.

"Sorry to keep you waiting," I said.

"Never mind. I was busy," was Maurice's reply.

"I could feel it, Maurice. Your work was not in vain."

Maurice drove silently, casting only a shy glance from time to time at the distraught passenger sitting beside him.

When we came to Pastor Daniel's house, we found a little sign on the door, written evidently by Esther, which read: "Please, dear friend, if at all possible, call between eight and nine in the morning or between five and six at night." It was now between five and six in the morning. Once more I had to act against the advice which I had given Daniel.

We knocked for a long time. It wasn't until Maurice knocked at the bedroom shutter that we got an answer.

"Who is it?"

"Some early callers, so undisciplined that they cannot keep your office hours."

"Walter!"

Daniel opened the door after quickly wrapping himself in his toga.

"Are you up already?"

"Nightshift," said Maurice.

Daniel looked from me to Fatma and from Fatma to Maurice. Indeed we were a strange-looking party.

"Come in."

I explained briefly the situation. Then we discussed who should call John. Fatma refused. Daniel volunteered, but Fatma was afraid that John would then know where she was. She pleaded with Daniel not to tell him.

"I doubt whether I'm the right one either in this case," I said. "At least I don't want to talk to him until Fatma has made up her mind.

He is very angry with me. . . . Fatma, did you ever talk to him about our telephone conversations?"

"Never!"

"But he knew that I had remarked about his dirty hands."

"He taped our telephone calls."

"All of them?"

"Yes."

"Also the one when you called here at the parsonage?"

"Yes, I discovered yesterday afternoon that he had a tape recorder connected to the telephone. I was afraid he would beat me when he came home. I escaped through a window and went to church before he got home from work. But then when I heard you speaking about the door with no handle inside, I felt even more locked in than at home and I lost all hope. I couldn't go to John, neither to my parents, nor to you."

Then Maurice volunteered to call John. There was no answer.

Esther came into the room, carrying her just-wakened baby. I introduced her to Fatma.

"Here is a very tired girl. She has to make a crucial decision. But she needs quietness in order to do this. First of all, though, she needs something to eat and then some sleep."

"She can have our guest room," Esther said.

"When she has rested, I wish you could have a good talk with her, Esther," I said.

Daniel smiled understandingly and Esther agreed.

"When is your wife coming?" she asked me.

"At four p.m.—that is, if the plane is on time."

"Good. Esther and I will pick you up at the hotel at three-thirty. If you like, we'll also have supper together—the four of us—at the airport restaurant."

I agreed, and took my leave with Maurice.

At first Maurice was very silent as he drove me back to my hotel. Then he asked:

"Did it ever happen to you before that your telephone calls were taped?"

"No, Maurice, I never even thought of this possibility."

"But he may have needed that criticism about his outward appearance. Maybe it was good for him."

"Maurice, if I didn't believe that God could use even our mistakes,

I'd have to quit this work immediately. The same is true of the remarks I made about the door without an inside handle. It was right— and still for Fatma at that moment, it was wrong."

"Still God used it with Fatma," Maurice replied.

"This is what we call 'grace,' Maurice. God plays billiards. We may push the ball in the wrong direction, yet God bounces it back and it ends up where it should—at the goal:"

We reached the hotel. Maurice, in his typical African politeness, accompanied me to the lobby. He didn't say anything. I had the feeling he was preoccupied. There in the lobby was John. He looked haggard and bleary-eyed. But he wore a suit.

We greeted each other and I told him what had happened. I gave him time to think. I could see that he was struggling with himself. Finally he said:

"I want to tell you one thing. Fatma is free to do what she wants to do. She can stay with me or leave."

"Thank you, John. I am glad to hear you say that."

I promised to keep him informed about Fatma. He said good-by coolly, but at least he departed in peace.

As I watched him leave the hotel, I couldn't help but feel sorry for him. What might be his story? Maybe he had had trouble in Europe. Maybe a fight with his boss or a broken engagement. Maybe a child out of wedlock or a divorce. Or maybe he wasn't even divorced and thought that distance would solve the problem. But distance never solves any problem, even if camouflaged by missionary zeal.

I turned to Maurice who was still deep in his thoughts and thanked him again for his help. We said good-night—or good-morning. When I went for my key at the desk, I asked the telephone operator not to put through any calls nor to allow any visitors until noon, for I had to get some sleep.

"But please be very polite and explain that I got up at three this morning. Most people who call have troubles."

"What is your work, sir?"

"Trying to help people with their troubles."

I had the feeling that she wanted to say something more, but the clerks at the desk were listening attentively. So she promised to do her best and took her place at the switchboard.

I went up to my room and fell asleep immediately.

8

IT WAS noon sharp when the telephone woke me up.

"I'm sorry to wake you, sir, but there's a call for you."

"That's all right. Were there many calls?"

"Yes, there were. And a couple who say they are Timothy and Miriam have been waiting here in the lobby since ten o'clock. They want to talk to you."

"Please tell them to wait until I have had a quick lunch. Then I will see them."

"Yes, sir. And one thing more. May I have a talk with you too?"

"Of course. Do you want to come up here?"

"It's against the hotel regulations for the personnel to enter the rooms of our guests. We would have to talk by phone."

"When are you off work?"

"At eleven p.m."

"All right, could you call me this evening before you leave?" Then she put the call through.

It was Esther. She reported that Fatma had rested and that she had

had a good talk with her. Fatma had not yet made up her mind what to do. She was still struggling.

"I told her she could stay with us for the time being."

"That's fine, Esther. Thank you. It reminds me of other suicide cases. A solution could have been found had they just waited a day longer. Staying with you is, of course, no final solution. It doesn't meet Fatma's deepest need. There's one thing, though, that I can't understand, Esther. I've read so much about the 'extended family' in Africa. But when it comes to an emergency like this, there doesn't seem to be a soul to help."

"The extended family still functions in the villages, but not in the city."

"But Fatma said she wanted to invite between three and four hundred people to her wedding."

"There is a difference whether you invite people to a wedding or whether you need them for help."

"True, but she called them 'friends.' Wouldn't there be one single real friend among them? This is what I can't understand."

"I shall try to talk to Fatma about it. I know this city quite well—it is no easy problem. But what did you mean when you said that having her stay with us is not yet meeting Fatma's deepest need? What is her deepest need? Do you think it is marriage?"

"No, not necessarily."

"Is it sex? Could it be that she is so wound up that she can't live without sex?"

"I don't think so. She's rather bored and disappointed as far as sex goes."

"What is she looking for, then?"

"A place."

"But I offered her a place in our home."

Typical, I thought. It's so hard for married people to understand the problems of those who are not married.

"Your offer is very good, Esther. For the time being, it is the best thing I could wish for Fatma. But this is not what I mean by 'place.' She needs a place where she belongs, which is her own, where her name is on the door and where she has her own furniture. A place where she is at home and where she can become a place—a place for others. I think she has been looking for such a place during her whole life, but she has never found it. She thought she would, when she let herself be taken in by men. All she found was a bed, but not a place. The lack of a place is one of the main motives for suicide."

Esther thought for awhile. Then she spoke: "In other words, unless someone marries her, she will never become happy."

She hadn't caught on yet.

"Not necessarily," I said patiently. "There are married couples who never become a place. And there are single people who have a place, who are a place. When you visit them you feel that you come into a place."

"And God? Where does God enter into all of this? Wouldn't you say that Fatma's deepest need is God?"

"Yes, Mrs. Pastor's wife."

"But you said that her deepest need is a place."

"It's the same. God is the only place there is. Those who find a place, find God. And those who find God, have found a place—regardless of where they are and regardless of whether they are married or single."

"I have to think that over. I think what we need just as much as marriage guidance is single life guidance," Esther said.

"Yes, I wholeheartedly agree. What's Fatma doing now?"

"She's writing. I don't know what. I didn't ask her."

"Good."

"What if she wants to go back to John?"

"Just let her go."

"And if she asks me to go along to pick up her things?"

"Then you go along, of course."

"But I . . ."

"And try to have a good talk with John at the same time. He needs help too. You are the logical person to help him. The door is shut for me in his case. I failed him."

"But Paster Walter, I have never done anything like that. I have no training."

"Just use your feminine intuition. Even if you had a lot of training, it wouldn't help you much without that. Counseling is an art, not a science."

"But I am a complete zero."

"So am I. We are both zeros, Esther. No one knows that better than I do after last night. But this is just when God can use us. He's the One in front of the zero. That's all that counts."

"Well, thank you, brother zero."

"Thank you, sister zero. And God bless you when you go to John's."

I hung up before she had a chance to reply.

After I had finished a quick lunch, Timothy and Miriam entered my room. There was a different air about them. They seemed to be more sure of themselves. Timothy was the first one to speak after they sat down together on the sofa. They had evidently planned it that way.

"We talked together," he said.

"Where?"

"In my brother's home."

"So there are places where you can talk after all."

"Yes, there are," he said with a smile. "We talked and we came to the conclusion that Miriam was not quite right yesterday when she said we had entered the triangle through the sex entrance. The truth is that we entered through the love entrance as well. We sort of switched back and forth between them. You see, we are a special case, an in-between case."

"I guess ninety-nine per cent of us are special in-between cases."

"At the beginning of our relationship I think there was love, genuine love. So, as you would say, we did enter through the love door. But then once we were inside, we went to the sex door. Pretty soon we almost forgot how we had come in. How shall I put it? We became one flesh, but not completely. We shared our bodies without sharing our minds. As soon as we realized this, we tried to switch back to love. But we couldn't find the door again."

"I was afraid to say 'no,'" Miriam finally said. "I thought that to love means never to say 'no.' And I was ashamed to blush."

"You are able to blush, Miriam," I interjected. "I saw that yesterday when you talked about the things not so beautiful."

"I shall respect your 'no's' and your blushings," Timothy said with a new assuring tone in his voice.

"All right," I said, "this is the diagnosis. What's the therapy?"

"We have two questions," Timothy answered. Again it was clear that they had carefully prepared the talk. "The first question is: Do you think that because of our differences in age, education, and character our marriage would fail in any case?"

"I wouldn't say that. Not in any case. In fact, I think it could be a real testimony if your marriage would succeed."

"How do you mean that?"

"It would be evident to everyone that yours is not a 'garden marriage' where the husband dominates his wife and respects her only as the bearer of his children. Miriam will never play the role of a garden. Either she marries as a partner or she doesn't marry. The people around you will notice that. This is what I mean by 'testimony.'"

I paused.

"But—" said Timothy.

"But what?"

"Well, you said that you did not think our marriage would fail in *any* case and that it *could* be a testimony, if it *would* succeed. So there must be a 'but.'"

I had to laugh. "True, if Miriam doesn't have enough tact and discretion and plays instead the card of her superiority and if you do not have enough self-denial and humility to accept her being ahead of you occasionally, then your marriage will be in danger. This can become the straw that breaks the camel's back. At least it will take very special effort."

"But do you think we could make it?" Timothy asked anxiously, while Miriam touched his hand.

"To be aware of the danger and to look it straight in the eye means that you have already half overcome it. However, it takes more than that to perform the extraordinary."

"But we are just very common people. There's nothing extraordinary about us."

"You are not extraordinary, but God may want to do something extraordinary with you."

"Do you mean that as Christians we could dare it?" Miriam concluded.

"I mean that the quality of the life you live with God will be decisive."

They were silent.

"This leads us to our second question." It was Timothy who picked up the conversation again. "Is it possible to start all over again?"

"What do you mean?"

"Starting from scratch, as if we had never entered the triangle. Approaching the love door slowly and then proceeding from there in both directions without skipping any steps."

"He means," Miriam added in her frank and direct way, "could we refrain from sex from now on until we are married, in spite of the fact that we went too far already?"

"It certainly will not be easy, for once you have started, the temptations will be greater. But I don't think it's impossible. With human strength alone it cannot be done. It takes special grace—an extraordinary power. I have seen others do it, though."

"And what was the outcome?"

"Usually it deepened their relationship. As soon as sex was out, they were able to get acquainted on a deeper level. But they helped each other, of course."

"How can we help each other?" Miriam wanted to know.

"Avoid certain situations. Give up your car rides alone at night, for example. Go out with other couples. Be honest. Don't pretend something is beautiful if it isn't."

"Won't this lead to tensions?"

"It certainly will. So what? Many sexual problems in our day arise because people think they, at all costs, have to avoid pain, renunciation, and tension. I believe that tension is something positive. It belongs to growing up and becoming mature. One day you will have to learn to stand up under tension—and a good time to learn it is before marriage."

"Does the tension keep on even within marriage?"

"Yes, it does. Those who have not learned to stand up under it before marriage will face a crisis during marriage. There is tension between all three angles of the triangle: between sex and love, between love and wedlock, and between wedlock and sex. It's like with a tent. It will be waterproof only as long as the canvas is tightened between the poles. As soon as the tension is gone, the tent sags."

Timothy and Miriam said nothing more. They said good-by and left hand in hand.

Daniel came to pick me up to go out to the airport. When we passed the desk, the telephone operator lifted up her head from the switchboard and greeted me with her eyes. I nodded to her. Suddenly, I remembered that I had made no room reservation for Ingrid.

We asked the clerk whether I could change to a double room. He explained that everything was filled up for the weekend.

"If only you had asked yesterday, or even this morning," he said.

"I really feel ashamed, Daniel. Here I've been so busy the whole week talking about marriage and sharing that I completely forgot to arrange for a room which I could share with my wife."

The clerk suggested a single room for her on the same floor, just across the hall from my room, and we settled for that.

"It will look at if we are not on good terms with each other," I said.

Daniel comforted me: "It does have the advantage that you can have talks separately. It was good that we had an extra guest room today when Esther talked with Fatma."

Esther was waiting for us in the car. I asked her who had watched the children when she was talking with Fatma and also during her long telephone conversation with me at noon.

"My husband did," she said proudly.

Daniel sighed audibly.

"Are you suffering, brother?"

"Terribly! If she goes on like this I don't know where it will end," he joked. Then he changed his tone of voice. "Seriously though, Walter, Esther is a different person since she has taken part in the work. I have a new wife."

"Who's watching the children now?" I asked.

"Fatma offered to take care of them so I could go with Daniel and you to the airport."

While we were driving to the airport, Daniel wanted to know whether I had given lessons in counseling to the telephone operator of the hotel.

"I tried to reach you this morning shortly after nine and the operator told me in a soft, kind voice: 'Sir, I know you must be a very troubled man. But please don't give up hope. The doctor is sleeping now. I'm not supposed to wake him up before noon. But I'm sure he will help you if you call again at that time.' "

We laughed wholeheartedly, all three of us.

"I just told her to be polite," I said. "But who would have thought that you would be the first 'client'? There were many calls today. I can't understand why no one has thought of starting a counseling service by telephone in this city."

In the meantime, we had arrived at the airport and learned that Ingrid's plane would be half an hour late. While we were waiting Daniel and Esther had a comment about my lecture the evening before.

"Last night we discussed the triangle with the slanted lines," Daniel began, "and the empty space created in that way, the 'vacuum in the relationship' as you said. But we know many engaged couples to whom this description does not apply. Their situation is different. They have known each other already for a long time. They are certain about their love. They have proved their faithfulness again and again. They've struggled together through many a crisis. Step by step they have grown in their expressions of love and at the same time in mutual responsibility. But due to some outward circumstances they are not yet able to get married. Maybe they don't have a place to live or they are both still in training, students, for example. Actually, there is no vacuum created, but only a very small space in between which separates them from the wedding and full physical union. Their case would look something like this."

Daniel took a card out of his jacket and drew a triangle on it with parallel lines where only the last one was slightly slanted:

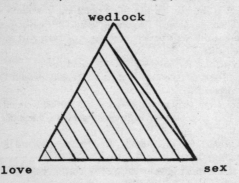

He explained further: "These couples say, 'It is not our fault that we have to begin our marriage before the wedding. We are forced to do so by outward circumstances. We know it's not ideal, but it seems for us to be the lesser evil. We take this risk which is better than the danger of repressing our natural desires, of becoming tense and nervous, and maybe even of losing each other.' Frankly, Walter, when I hear them talk, I must admit they do have a point. By waiting for such a long time they may disturb the dynamic play of forces more than by giving themselves to each other before the wedding."

"This is really the most difficult as well as the most widely disputed case," I replied. "No one on the outside has a right to judge or even condemn them."

"But don't some people claim that premarital sex makes marriages happier?" Esther wanted to know.

"Personally," I replied, "I know of no couple who have ever claimed that their marriage would have failed had they not consummated it before the wedding. I know some couples who would say that premarital sex has not done any damage to their marriage. But I know far more couples who, upon looking back, view it in a different light, although they began their marriage before the wedding with the best of arguments."

"We read your book, *I Loved a Girl*. Are François and Cecile among the latter?" Daniel asked.

"I believe so. They both thought that the high bride price for Cecile which François couldn't pay justified their crossing the 'small in-between space' in the triangle. Today I think they wished they had waited."

"But what would you say to such a couple?"

"Well, first of all, I would check with them all their reasons for not getting married. Sometimes the real motive is only false pride. They are too proud to start their wedded life with just a table and a bed. Why not? It may even be good to rough it a little in the beginning. I would tell them, if you start at the bottom, then you can only go upward."

"So you would even encourage them to begin in a small rented room with a hot plate as a kitchen stove?"

"I think that postponing the wedding just because one does not have a new bedroom suite is foolish."

"The trouble here is," Daniel explained, "many of our church members don't get married because they cannot afford the white man's clothes—a dark suit for the bridegroom and a satin wedding dress for the bride. Others delay because they think they have to give the traditional wedding feast which is expensive."

"This makes me even more convinced that we should encourage simple weddings!" I exclaimed. "An engaged couple who have tested their love and faithfulness for an ample period of time should be encouraged by their family to celebrate their wedding as soon as possible."

"And what if that isn't possible?" Daniel insisted.

"Then you must call their attention to the fact that although they may solve one problem through their physical surrender—that of releasing their sexual tension—there are many new problems coming up."

"And what are the main problems for such a couple?" Esther asked as we waited.

"The couple have to be reminded that there is no point of return. The revolving door is stationary from that day on. Also, if the couple have no place of their own, mutual adjustment is difficult. It is the girl who suffers more from the feeling of not being sheltered than the young man, and this may hinder her from reaching full sexual satisfaction."

"And how about contraceptives?" Esther asked.

"Often they haven't even thought of this when making their decision. They soon recognize that there is no ideal solution to this problem and that a compromise has to be made with every method. It's not so easy to come together without living together."

Ingrid's plane had arrived at last. The first passengers appeared.

Then I saw my wife. Upright and queenly she moved slowly down the steps. She was wearing a light brown suit with a green scarf tucked in at the neckline. Her favorite colors, I thought.

As I watched her striding with measured steps the distance between the plane and the building, swinging slightly her long arms which betrayed her Swedish descent, I felt proud to be married to this fashionable lady. Daniel was silent.

Ingrid's face was fresh and radiant as she waved to us. Unbelievable that the same person had written such a depressing letter a few days ago, I thought.

I took a look at her hand baggage and hoped secretly that she had remembered what I had forgotten: gifts for Daniel and Esther.

After we had all exchanged affectionate greetings, we went to the airport restaurant. We sat down, the four of us, around a table and ordered a meal. As we waited, Ingrid distributed gifts for everyone: a blouse for Esther, a tie for Daniel, a large calendar with colored pictures of the Austrian Alps for their home, small toys for the children.

The surprise gifts broke the ice fast. Before long we were conversing like old friends. I appreciated the ease with which Ingrid made contact.

They wanted to know if Americans had the same problems as Africans, if they needed the marriage triangle as much as they did.

Daniel said he had read about the "swinging" clubs in the States where total sexual freedom reigns. Husband and wife go there together, pair off with whomever they want, without getting emotionally involved, and then leave again as husband and wife. But the managers of these clubs have noticed that a couple can't keep it up for very long. Something in them seems to rebel.

"Yes," Ingrid said, "they think it's an escape from what they call 'monotonous monogamy,' but the result is usually more emptiness and loneliness. Americans need the triangle as much as Africans do. We have to show that monogamy can be an exciting adventure, integrating both sex and love into marriage. There's nothing more boring than adultery, nothing more empty than divorce."

Esther had a vision. "It would be great if we could once proclaim this message together, all four of us, an African and a European-American couple as a team."

"Yes, it would be a tremendous help if Africans could hear this message out of an African mouth," I agreed.

"But it would be still more striking for Americans and Europeans to hear this message out of an African mouth," Ingrid added.

"I think so too," I answered, adding, with a knowing glance toward Esther, "providing you are honest zeros—neither pumped up, wanting to be a little bit more than just zero, nor shrunken up, wanting to be a little bit less. The shrunken zeros want to appear humble in the eyes of others. You see, inferiority feelings often cover up hidden pride."

"Don't you dare give my wife counseling lessons again," Daniel protested laughingly. He turned to Ingrid: "Your husband made my wife a pastor and me a children's nurse. I tell you it's enough to have one pastor in our family."

"They have the same problem as we do, Ingrid," I explained, "never an undisturbed moment, many interruptions, and the constant conflict between their marriage and their work. He has time to listen to everyone's troubles, but not to those of his wife. It sounds familiar, doesn't it?"

Ingrid thought for a moment. Then she said: "There's only one solution. You need a hiding place. Some place out of town where no one can find you and which nobody knows about. There you should go together once a week for a whole day or at least half a day."

Esther's face lit up. "I know where we could go," she said.

"Where?" Daniel wanted to know.

"I'll tell you when we are alone," she said with a roguish smile. "Nobody else is supposed to know it."

"Walter sometimes goes to a Catholic monastery when he wants to work undisturbed," Ingrid said.

"Yes, that's true," I said, "and then I always envy the priests for not being married."

Esther wanted to know whether I was serious.

"Sure he is," Daniel replied in my stead. "I think every married man has moments when he wishes he were single."

Daniel motioned to the waiter for the bill. He insisted on paying it himself. We were careful not to refuse his African hospitality, although I knew that, with his small salary, this was a real sacrifice.

As we drove from the airport to the hotel, the two ladies sat in the back seat. Esther thanked Ingrid again for the good advice concerning the hiding place.

"I read a book once," Daniel said to me while Ingrid and Esther talked together, "in which the author advises the counselor not to give advice."

"That's also an advice, isn't it?"

"Yes, but he says that to give advice means to direct people. One should not do that."

"You can't avoid it, Daniel. Not to direct is also a way of directing— perhaps the most clever way. I agree with Paul Tournier who claims that no one can be really morally neutral, and that although we say nothing openly, our secret reflections and judgments do not escape the other one's intuition.*

"Even if you say nothing, he will imagine what you are thinking and he will spend a lot of time thinking about what he thinks you are thinking. This way he may come to entirely wrong conclusions. I believe it's more honest and less dangerous to share frankly with the other person your opinion—and then, of course, give him the freedom to accept it or not."

"But, Walter, the author said that if you give advice you are like one who is sitting on the safe bank of a river talking to someone who is in the water. Instead, you should jump in and swim with him."

"On the contrary," I replied, "if you don't give any advice, you stay

---

* Cf. Paul Tournier, *A Place for You* (New York: Harper & Row, 1968), p. 85.

out of the water. But if you give advice, it's like jumping in. If the other one accepts and follows your advice, you are responsible. You are linked together. You swim right along with him."

We arrived at the hotel and said good-by to Esther and Daniel.

"Please call me up when you get home," I said to Daniel, "and tell me how Fatma is."

I was glad that there was no lecture this evening. I still was tired from last night.

When we were alone in my room, I took Ingrid in my arms. Tears came to her eyes. "It's all too much," she said.

"How did you leave the children?" I asked.

"They're all fine. I took the boys back to their boarding school on Thursday. Here's a letter from David for you."

I read the sprawling lines of my twelve-year-old son: "Last night I had a strange dream. I dreamt that I went with you and Mommy to Africa. You asked me what my motto was. I thought awhile and then the words of the song came to me: *Gehe mit dem Herrn allewege* ['Go with the Lord all the way']."

This giving up of our children causes us to discover them in a new way, I thought, and maybe even aids their inner growth.

"But wasn't it hard on little Ruthy when you left? She's only eight," I said to Ingrid.

"She was all excited about staying with our neighbors while I'm on this trip. She had put your old sea captain's cap on her stuffed elephant so she wouldn't be lonely for you. And do you know the last thing she said to me? 'Mommy, don't be sad because you're not going to see me. You know the days will go by fast!' I often think they are braver than their mother. Tell me, how did your lectures go?"

"Ask the people who heard them, not me."

"Esther already told me about them in the car. I wasn't surprised. I knew even before I started out on this trip that God was using you."

We sat down together on the sofa where Miriam and Timothy had been just a few hours before.

"Your complaining letters don't make it easier for me, you know."

"I didn't mean to complain. I just wanted to share the facts."

"But when you share these facts, I feel accused. It's as if you were saying that it's my fault that I leave you alone. That I don't love you enough."

"That's not what I wanted to . . ."

"Don't you understand that I need a different kind of letter when I do this work?"

"Yes, I know it so well, but I can't write you other letters unless I am first able to share how I really feel. When I am so helpless, I don't know what else to do. I have no one to talk to about my innermost feelings when you are away. If I can't write them to you, I don't know what would happen."

Ingrid didn't try to hold back her tears anymore. She put her head on my lap and sobbed quietly. Gone was the queenly lady. All that was left was the sensitive child.

The telephone rang. I reached for the receiver while my left hand kept stroking her hair. It was Daniel.

"I just wanted to congratulate you on your wife," he said. "You know, she strikes me as an angel. I never had this impression about anyone else. First I thought, she isn't real. But she is. She radiates something."

"Yes," I said, while Ingrid continued to weep, her head buried in my lap.

"When she enters a room, the room becomes different. Esther too is completely taken by her."

"Thank you. Sometimes I wonder how a clumsy, bearish fellow as I am could have found such a wife."

Ingrid lifted up her head, but I pressed it down tenderly.

"But how is Fatma?"

"She's fine. When we came home we found her playing with the children and then she ate supper with them. She seems to be at peace with herself. It looks as though she has made up her mind, but I refrained from giving her any advice."

"Don't worry," I said, "she knows anyway what you want her to do."

"She said she's written a letter to you, but it isn't finished yet. She wants to give it to you tomorrow after the service. But Walter, the reason for my calling is that the church is filling up again. People are streaming in. You must come and give us a lecture tonight too."

"Didn't you announce that there would be no meeting tonight?"

"Yes, I did. But the people have come anyway. Maybe I didn't make it clear enough. There are many newcomers. I can't just send them home. You have to come, Walter."

"I just can't, Daniel."

"Are you trying to teach me how to say 'no'?"

"Couldn't Ingrid come instead of me?"

Ingrid raised her head with a start and sat up straight.

"Just let me ask her."

Ingrid shook her head violently.

"She okayed it," I said. "Pick her up in fifteen minutes."

Ingrid grabbed the receiver out of my hand, but I had already pressed down the hook and thus cut off the call.

"But I don't have anything prepared," Ingrid said. I knew her too well to be worried about that and concluded from the tone of her voice that her defense was breaking down.

"Just let them ask questions," I suggested. "I'm sure they will have hundreds once you have won their confidence, and that's not hard for you. But hurry up and change. They will pick you up soon."

She looked around the room. "Is that supposed to be a double bed?"

"Ingrid, I'm sorry. They didn't have a double room free for tonight. So I had to take another single room for you. It's just across the hall from this one."

She didn't say anything, but I could see the struggle she had in accepting this fact.

"It might even be better this way," I said, "just in case someone wants to have a private talk with you after the meeting."

"All right," she said, "it doesn't matter." Then she went to her room to get ready. But again I knew her too well. The tone of her voice indicated that to her it mattered very much.

After Ingrid had left I tried to work on my sermon. My text was Ephesians 5:21-33.

"Husbands, love your wives, as Christ loved the church," was the key verse. How did Christ love the church? He served her, I thought. He did not come to be served, but to serve. He made himself subject to her, gave himself up for her.

This cast a new light for me on the verse which all husbands hail and all wives abhor: "Wives, be subject to your husbands." It dawned on me that then the submission of the wife is only a submission in response to the submission of her husband. "Be subject to one another."

Yes, but how? Who has ever achieved this balance? It seems to be a daily assignment.

The telephone rang again. It was the operator, but this time she was calling in her own right.

"You gave me permission to call you, sir!"

"Yes, I did. What's your problem?"

"My husband drinks."

"Why?"

"I don't know."

"You should know. There must be a hole somewhere in his life."

"A hole?"

"Yes, a drunkard always tries to fill a hole, an empty container. There must be a deficiency somewhere, an emptiness in his life."

"I have no idea."

"Do you have children?"

"Yes, one child."

"How old is your child?"

"Almost four."

"Doesn't your husband want another child?"

"Yes, but if he drinks, I have to work and then I can't afford another one."

"Why don't you make a bargain with him?"

"A bargain?"

"Yes, real hard bargaining belongs to marriage too."

"All right. What should we bargain about?"

"He stops drinking and you agree to have another baby."

"Thank you, sir. I won't forget our talk."

"And now I want to give you another number to call."

"Yes, please."

"Four thirteen."

"One digit is lacking. Every telephone number in this city has four digits."

"It's a number for you to call when you need it."

"For me?"

"Yes, do you have a Bible?"

"I can find one."

"Then call Philippians four thirteen in case of need: 'I can do all things in him who strengthens me.' " There was silence.

I hung up. Again I had given advice, I thought. I am an impossible counselor, a poor husband, and a pastor without a sermon. I sat in front of my blank sheet of paper and couldn't write a line. It was the same feeling I had had on the first evening here.

When Ingrid came back from the church, I still hadn't written one word of my sermon. I could just as well have gone with her.

"How did it go?" I asked her.

"Very well, considering the circumstances. After Daniel introduced me as your wife and the mother of our three sons and two daughters, he encouraged them to ask questions about anything they wanted. He told them not to be ashamed to call things by name which God was not ashamed to create. That did it. The questions broke loose like a flood. We could have gone on for hours."

"What were they all about?"

"Mostly about women and their biological functions. When I explained the ovarian cycle and the changes it brings in a woman's body as well as in her emotions, one man stood up and asked: 'Is this why my wife is never the same two days in a row?'

"Another wanted to know what to do when his wife is pregnant and craves strange things, which sometimes cost a lot of money. Should he just laugh at her, or should he try to get the things for her?"

"I know already what you answered. You told them the story about the apples when we were in Cameroun and you were pregnant with Kathy. And you described how your model husband made a special trip to the airport to meet the plane from Europe in order to buy two pounds of expensive apples . . ."

"Yes, and . . ."

"And that your heart melts with love for me every time you think of those apples and . . ."

"And how thankful I am to have such an understanding husband!"

"I can imagine what you said. It's a good thing I wasn't present. What else did they ask you?"

"They wanted to know where twins come from, what causes a miscarriage, whether a man can sleep with his wife when she's pregnant, why so many mothers die in childbirth—they were all good questions."

"Oh, sister, I'm glad you were there and not I. Could you answer them all?"

"Fortunately I had my teaching charts along. I used the one with the enlarged picture of the female reproductive organs in order to explain how a baby is conceived."

"You mean you hung it up?"

"Of course. Daniel had a little stand and we hung it on that, right in front of the altar where all the people could see it."

"You know, Ingrid, before I gave my first lecture, Daniel warned me about using the word 'sex.' And now you hang the uterus in front of the altar. They've come a long way, I'd say."

"They didn't seem to mind at all. Daniel had to call on Esther, though, to help him interpret when we talked about the female organs. She told me afterward how she had said it in their mother tongue. The uterus she called 'the house of the baby,' the ovaries she called 'the storehouse of the eggs,' and the vagina she explained as being 'the road for birth.'

"After I had explained about conception and the growth of a baby in the womb, one of the older men stood up. In his hand he had a closed envelope. He said he had a question which burned like fire in his heart. 'If I give you this closed envelope,' he said, 'and there's a letter inside it, can you tell me what the letter says while the envelope is still closed?' I had to admit I couldn't. 'All right then,' he said. 'How can you know what it looks like inside a woman's body, in a woman's stomach?' That was the term he used."

"Did you have the feeling that they believed you, that they accepted what you said?"

"For the most part, yes. But they had a hard time when I talked about breastfeeding. They are thoroughly convinced that if a breast-feeding mother has intercourse with her husband, her milk will be spoiled and the baby will get sick, perhaps even die. And since they breastfeed their babies at least until they start to walk, intercourse is forbidden for one year, sometimes two years after the birth of a child."

"Yes, I know. I find this belief wherever I go in Africa."

"It never dawned on me to what degree a false biological conception can have ethical consequences. If a couple don't dare to have inter-course for two years after the baby, they must become polygamous."

"Or the husband goes to a prostitute and catches a disease. Then the vicious circle starts," I added.

"I think it's here where missions have failed. Instead of moralizing, we should have given information."

"Ingrid," I said, putting my hands on her shoulders and looking into her eyes, "I'm so thankful for you. You are a good team partner. I wonder if you would help me to preach tomorrow."

"You mean in the pulpit? Never!"

"You can stand down below if you want. But it would be wonderful if you could tell the story of Mother Gerda as a part of my sermon."

"I shall see. By the way, I read something wonderful in the plane which I would like so much to share with you."

"Ingrid, please understand, not now! I haven't done anything on my sermon yet."

Ingrid hesitated, but only for a second. Then she said: "All right. I'm sorry you have no time. I have to go anyway. There's a girl waiting to talk to me. Her name is Miriam. She says she's engaged. She was very interested when I explained the symptoms of ovulation and wants to ask me some more questions about it. It's good she's starting now to get acquainted with her cycle, because after the wedding it's actually too late to start determining her fertile and infertile days."

"I'm so glad you are doing that, Ingrid. I couldn't. That's why I need you as a co-worker."

"When do we have to get up tomorrow?"

"Seven o'clock at the latest. The service starts at nine and I'd like to go over my message with you first. We have to pack too. Our plane leaves at noon sharp. We won't have time to come back to the hotel after the service, but will have to go directly from the church to the airport."

I kissed her good-night and she left.

9

THE NEXT MORNING I got up at six and packed my two suitcases. Shortly before seven, I called Ingrid's room to see whether she was awake. She said she would open the door. I entered her room and sat down at her bedside. She had her eyes shut, but I saw that her cheeks were wet with tears.

"Didn't you sleep well?"

She shook her head, but didn't say anything.

"But Ingrid, what's wrong? We were so happy last night. You had such a great evening. Then I kissed you good-night . . ."

"No, you didn't."

"Yes, I did."

"That's not what I call a kiss—just a little peck. I had so hoped you would come over to my room afterward."

"Ingrid, don't be foolish. I knew you were having a talk with Miriam and I didn't want to disturb you. Besides, I had work to do on my sermon."

"There you have it: Your sermon is more important than anything else."

"But I have to preach on marriage today."

"I wonder what you'll have to say. You don't understand a woman. You don't know what marriage is. If you only knew how hard it is to be married to you. Sometimes I think we haven't made any progress at all in these eighteen years."

Now it was I who was silent.

Ingrid continued: "When you said you had no time to listen to what I wanted to read to you, I felt as if you had slapped me."

She paused. When I said nothing, she went on: "I got the message from you: 'Don't bother me!' All night I struggled with the temptation to believe that almost anything or anyone else is more important in your life than I am. And still I couldn't overcome my desire just to be alone with you."

"But Ingrid, listen. You're not thankful at all. We've been led in a wonderful way up to this point. This morning there's a church full of people who are awaiting a message on marriage from us. We can travel together, work together. Remember how we started our married life?"

"Yes, in a little attic room with a slanted wall, where there was barely room for both of us to stand up straight. Our kitchen was an electric plate on the washstand. Last night I kept wishing we were back in that room together instead of living in two fancy hotel rooms."

"You really are ungrateful."

"No, I'm just a woman. That's what you don't understand. You can write and talk about marriage all you want, but sometimes I think you haven't even understood the ground rules. For you, I'm just a team partner, a co-worker, a showpiece—but not your wife."

I got up from her bedside, went to the window and looked out, my back turned to her.

Without turning around I said: "But Ingrid, after all, we are married. We are together—"

"Yes," she interrupted, "we are together, but always *unterwegs,* en route, never in a relaxed atmosphere and almost never together in the shelteredness of our home."

"Everything entails a sacrifice," I said.

"All I know," Ingrid replied, "is that if fruit comes from your ministry, then it is because it has cost tears and travail."

"But you say this with bitterness."

"I'm sorry, but my feelings are numb. I don't have the strength to rejoice."

I kept looking out of the window. I discovered the steeple of the church. The bell would be ringing now. Pretty soon we would be picked up for the service. It was impossible for me to preach now, I thought. I have no message. Always when I am happiest, she does that, she tears down everything.

"Now you are wishing you were a Catholic priest," Ingrid said.

I whirled around. "Yes I do," I said without trying to hide the scorn in my voice.

" 'Monogamy can be an exciting adventure,' " Ingrid retorted, and I knew she was aware that it would hurt me.

"You know," I said, "if you were Esther, I would know exactly what to tell you. But because you're my wife, I am helpless."

"And if you were Daniel, I would know what to tell you too, but because . . ." Instead of continuing, the trace of a smile crossed her face.

I sat down at her bedside again. The minutes passed. No one to spread my tent, I thought. It had been a week of victories: Maurice, Miriam, Daniel, Fatma. And now I stood here as the defeated one. Who would help me to spread my own tent?

At last the quietness was interrupted by the ringing of the telephone. "The gentleman who always picks you up is here."

Maurice was on the line. "Shall I come up to help you with your baggage?"

"Maurice, listen, we aren't ready yet. Ingrid is still in bed."

"Is she sick?"

"No, that is, yes. In a way."

"What's the matter?"

"Our tent broke down."

"You mean you . . ."

"Yes, we have a marriage crisis."

"You're joking. Is it possible for a marriage counselor also to have a marriage crisis?"

"That's just like asking, Is it possible for a doctor to fall ill?"

"What can I do?"

"Just wait. Could you order coffee and rolls for us and have them sent up to my wife's room? I'll call you back as soon as possible."

I hung up. I knew that Maurice would pray. God had heard his prayers for me once before.

Ingrid was calm now. I bent over her and took her head in my arms.

"I want to share my ministry with you, but it actually makes it harder, not easier. If only I didn't have to preach on 'Husbands, love your wives, as Christ loved the church'!"

Ingrid tried to smile. "What did you mean when you said 'Our tent broke down'?"

"One of the girls who came to the lectures, Fatma is her name, saw my triangle. She said it reminded her of a tent."

"A tent!" Ingrid said thoughtfully. "What a good idea. That's a picture every woman can understand. It almost reconciles me to your very angular triangle with all its sharp corners."

"I knew you would like it."

"Remember when we were camping once, just the two of us, and at night a storm came up and our tent broke down?"

"Yes, I remember. The tent poles were broken and we had to spend the night covered just by the canvas while the storm raged around us."

"Exactly. The tent broke down, but we were still covered, even if it was a broken tent."

"And now? Aren't we still covered even now? Aren't we still married?"

Instead of answering, Ingrid said: "You see, Walter, this is what I wanted you to do last night—to come into my room and cover me with the blanket."

I sighed with relief and yet I was burdened at the same time. "Well, Ingrid, I could have done that, easily and gladly. But you see, this is precisely what makes me feel insecure and fearful—that you make everything depend upon one little gesture—our marriage, our work, our message, our ministry."

"It isn't a little gesture to me. It's full of meaning. It would have made me feel sheltered and secure in your love."

The maid brought Ingrid's breakfast tray.

"Who's this Maurice you were talking to?" Ingrid asked as we drank our coffee.

"He works for a construction company. He's neither a psychologist nor a theologian. Besides that, he's still a bachelor. Shall I call him to come up and be our arbitrator? He's very wise."

"It's all right with me," Ingrid said to my surprise.

It was quite a step for both of us—to come here all the way from Europe in order to help Africans with their marriage problems and then to ask an African to help us. But it was good for us. To be helped is the best, if not the only way, to learn how to help others.

Maurice came at once. He looked at us curiously as he entered the room. He probably had expected a different scene. It didn't exactly look like a serious crisis. Ingrid and I were sitting together on the couch and I was holding her hand.

He took a chair and said nothing. It was clear that he did not know what to say.

"Last night," I began, "I committed all the errors which I advise other husbands not to commit. I talked only about my work. I told my wife to give a message in church and to prepare another one for this morning. I forgot to kiss her good-night properly."

"And he didn't even say that he loves me."

"That's right. I didn't say that I love her and I didn't cover her with a blanket."

"The last thing he told me yesterday evening," Ingrid added, "was that I had to get up at seven and have all the baggage ready before church."

Ingrid finally succeeded in smiling. "And he had no time to listen when I wanted to read him something."

"She's right. Instead, I prepared a sermon about how husbands should love their wives."

"You see," she explained, "it irritated me that he had time for everyone else, but not for me; that everyone else had access to him, even the telephone operator."

Maurice was puzzled. Then he picked up the word "operator" and said to Ingrid, though as kindly as possible:

"I talked with the operator while I was waiting downstairs. Your husband told her last night that marriage is sometimes real hard bargaining. Why don't you make a bargain with Walter? He listens to you while you read to him that which you wanted to share and then it's his turn to say what he wants."

Without further comment, Ingrid picked up the little booklet on her night table. It was printed by a Catholic brotherhood in Switzerland and in it was an essay on tenderness by a German author, Karl Krolow. She read the paragraph she had underlined:

"Tenderness is the pianissimo of the heart, softer than a pulse beat during sleep. For tenderness never sleeps. It is wide awake, attentive in the light of noon-day and diving into the black waters of midnight. It is restless and beautiful and we can gladly entrust our innermost feelings to it. . . ."*

I looked at my wife and loved her. So this was what she wanted to share! Now I understood her.

"Walter's turn to say what he wants from his wife." Maurice was doing a good job as umpire.

I was ready: "I want her to give her message this morning in church about Mother Gerda."

Ingrid agreed. "I have no strength now to build up our tent again," she said, "but I can crawl into His tent and He will give me the shelter I need."

"It's nine o'clock," Maurice said. "The service is starting. We have no time to wait for Ingrid. We can barely make it before it is time for you to preach."

"Why don't you take me to the church, Maurice, and then return and pick up Ingrid and our baggage. I will preach until she comes and then turn it over to her."

As we drove, Maurice said that he still had a question, but he would ask it after the service on our way to the airport.

When we entered the church the congregation was already singing the pulpit hymn. The pews were packed again, but a different atmosphere reigned than during the evening lectures. People sat stiff and upright, their faces almost solemn. This was their worship service. They were ready to stand before God, to be addressed by Him in a special way.

We had to go to the pulpit immediately. What a difference compared with the first night, I thought as I looked over the velvet carpet of black hair. I felt a bond between the congregation and me as if we were one big family. There was an openness and receptiveness, something in the air as if hundreds of empty hands were being held up, waiting to be filled.

I was poorer than ever before. Yet I felt that I had something—I was the bearer of a message and at the same time, the message bore me up.

* *"Zärtlichkeit"* ["Tenderness"], *Ferment Jahrbuch*, 1969, Pallottiner Verlag, Gossau, Switzerland.

I decided to choose only verses 25 to 32 of Ephesians 5 and read Paul's message:

"Husbands, love your wives, as Christ loved the church and gave himself up for her, that he might sanctify her, having cleansed her by the washing of water with the word, that he might present the church to himself in splendor, without spot or wrinkle or any such thing, that she might be holy and without blemish. Even so husbands should love their wives as their own bodies. He who loves his wife loves himself. For no man ever hates his own flesh, but nourishes and cherishes it, as Christ does the church, because we are members of his body! 'For this reason a man shall leave his father and mother and be joined to his wife, and the two shall become one.' This is a great mystery, and I take it to mean Christ and the church."

Daniel read it too in the national language and then interpreted my sermon sentence by sentence, quietly and effortlessly. It was again as if we were speaking out of one mouth.

"During the last four days we have studied the triangle of marriage: leaving, cleaving, becoming one flesh.

"In the text I just read, the Apostle Paul adds a new dimension to this triangle. He says: 'This is a great mystery.'

"This statement is found in an in-between place in this text. It refers to the previous verse and points to the following one at the same time.

"Paul says: When a man leaves father and mother—this is a great mystery. When a man cleaves to his wife—this is a great mystery. When the two become one—this is a great mystery.

"Indeed it is. All of us have been touched this week. We have been touched by the depth of this mystery. We have been touched by the power of God's Word. The Bible verse we studied has been like a hammer which breaks rocks into pieces in our midst. But it has equipped all of us with new hope."

Fatma, Miriam, and Esther were sitting together on the women's side. I couldn't help but glance at them for a moment. There was a trace of joy on all three faces: new vision and new depth on Esther's; assurance and resolve on Miriam's; the touch of healing on Fatma's.

"Indeed," I continued, "this is a great mystery. But then Paul continues: 'I take it to mean Christ and the church.'

"Paul says: A man leaves his father and mother—I speak about Christ. A man cleaves to his wife—I speak about Christ. The two become one—I speak about Christ."

I unfolded my wooden triangle again.

"In other words: The deepest mystery of our triangle is Jesus Christ himself. When I gave you the triangle—leaving, cleaving, one flesh—as a guide for marriage, I gave you nothing else, no one else as a guide except Jesus Christ himself.

"A man leaves his father—I talk about Christ.

"Because he loves us, Christ left his father at Christmas. He became man. A child in the manger. Did not count equality with God a thing to be grasped. Emptied himself. Humbled himself. Was obedient even unto death, even death on a cross.

"A man leaves his mother—I talk about Christ.

"Because he loves us, Christ left his mother on Good Friday. When he was on the cross he gave his mother another son. He said to her: 'Woman, behold your son' and to John 'Behold your mother.'

"A man cleaves to his wife—I talk about Christ.

"Because he loves us, Christ cleaves to us, the Church, his bride, cleaves to us faithfully, inseparably.

"The Bible conceives of the alliance between Christ and the Church as a marriage. 'For the marriage of the Lamb has come, and his Bride made herself ready' (Rev. 19:7). 'I saw the holy city . . . prepared as a bride adorned for her husband' (Rev. 21:2).

"It is not always a marriage without a crisis. The Church is sometimes a difficult wife. We are ungrateful, disobedient, unfaithful to Christ. We refuse to be subject to him.

"Once he had to say to the Church in Sardis: 'Because you are lukewarm, and neither cold nor hot, I will spew you out of my mouth' (Rev. 3:16).

"True love does not shy away from hard words.

"But Christ never walks out on his wife completely, even if she deserved it over and over. He never goes farther away than the door. 'Behold, I stand at the door and knock.'

" 'Husbands, love your wives, as Christ loved the church. . . .'

"He is always ready with his forgiveness. He sanctified her. He cleansed her. He washed her. Just as a slave washes the feet of his master. He made her appear in splendor. Without spot. Without wrinkle. Without blemish. There can never be a divorce between Christ and his Church. He gave himself up for her. For this unsubmissive, difficult wife, he gave himself up.

" 'Husbands, love your wives, as Christ loved the church.'

"And since Paul refers to Christ when he states: 'The two shall become one,' we can also say: 'Wives, love your husbands, as Christ loved the church.' For if they are one in Christ, what is true about one is true about the other.

"The two become one—I talk about Christ.

"Because he loves us, he becomes one with us, just as the head and body are one.

"He shares everything with us.

"Whatever is ours becomes his. Our poverty becomes his poverty. Our fear becomes his fear. Our suffering becomes his suffering. Our guilt becomes his guilt. Our punishment becomes his punishment. Our death becomes his death.

"Whatever is his becomes ours. His riches become our riches. His peace becomes our peace. His joy becomes our joy. His forgiveness becomes our forgiveness. His innocence becomes our innocence. His life becomes our life.

"And he becomes one flesh with us in a very concrete sense, becomes physically part of us, in Holy Communion.

"The triangle of marriage points to Jesus Christ, reveals what he has done for us. I have talked to you about marriage all week. But in a deeper sense I have talked to you about Christ all week. And I would like to say to you, as Paul did in I Corinthians 2:2: 'For I decided to know nothing among you except Jesus Christ and him crucified.' "

Daniel's voice became warmer and warmer. I could feel how he put himself completely into every word that he translated. It was as if he anticipated everything I was going to say, as if he took the words out of my mouth even before I had pronounced them. With all his heart he wanted his congregation to grasp this message.

"You may forget many things which my wife and I said about marriage," I continued, "but one thing please do not forget:

"That Christ left his father for you, because he loves you, loves you personally.

"That Christ left his mother for you, because he loves you, loves every one of you.

"That Christ wants to cleave to you, because he loves you, loves you in spite of your not cleaving to him.

"That Christ wants to become one with you, one flesh, in a very intimate and personal way, because he loves you, loves you eternally."

The church was completely silent. Suddenly, something unexpected happened. A man in one of the front pews stood up and started to sing aloud. Before I knew it, the whole congregation joined in and sang from the depths of their hearts.

I looked at Daniel. "Do they want me to quit?"

"No," he whispered, "this means that they are glad about your message. They must express their joy. At the same time they want to give you some rest so that you can continue with new power."

Truly I had never preached to such a considerate church audience.

"What do they sing?" I asked Daniel.

"They are praising the love of God," he answered.

After they had finished, I began again, praying in my heart for a special word to meet Fatma's need.

"One of you has seen the picture of a tent in the triangle of marriage. This has given me a new insight into the mystery of marriage.

"After this earth has passed away and every tear has been wiped from our eyes, the Bible describes the new creation. Then God and His people will dwell together as closely as a married couple under the shelter of a tent: 'Behold, the tent of God is with men. He will dwell with them' (Rev. 21:3).

"But before this hour comes, Christ is God's tent among us, a tent with the three poles: leaving, cleaving, one flesh. Therefore, the message of our tent is not only a message for married people. In Christ, all those who are unmarried are included under the cover of God's tent as well. For Christ left his father and mother for them too; he cleaves to them too; he becomes one with them too.

"In Christ their life receives purpose and fulfillment, freedom and joy. In Christ they find their place, their tent.

"Since Jesus Christ came into this world, there is no one without a tent."

At this moment the main door at the back of the church was opened and Ingrid and Maurice entered. The people turned their heads to look at them. I took advantage of the pause and said:

"Would you like me to call on my wife to tell you a story?"

They were very much in agreement.

"Ingrid, please tell us the story of Mother Gerda as an example of a marriage under the cover of God's tent."

Daniel motioned to Esther to translate for Ingrid. The two women stood in the front of the church in the center aisle, while Daniel and I remained standing in the pulpit.

I sensed immediately that Ingrid was again herself. There was no sign on her face of the sleepless night and the tears. Her eyes sought contact with the audience and found it. She had passed through the valley, and this seemed to give her special authority at this moment.

"The pastor who performed the wedding ceremony for my husband and me had seven children," she began. "After thirty years of marriage, his wife became very sick. She had a brain tumor. This meant that sometimes she could not think clearly. A strange desire would cause her to run away from home. So her husband had to watch over her day and night.

"As her sickness grew worse, she could walk and talk only with great difficulty. Her husband had to help her with everything. He had to feed her, wash her, dress her.

"This went on for fifteen years."

An audible expression of amazement and compassion went through the church. Ingrid continued:

"Whenever his friends suggested that he put his wife into a home or hospital for incurable patients, the pastor always refused. 'She is my wife and the mother of our seven children,' he would say. 'I cannot give her into a home or hospital.'

"Shortly before her death, I visited her. She could talk a little bit on that day. And this is what she said to me: 'Ingrid, whenever you and Walter talk about marriage I want you to tell the people that my husband loves me today just as he loved me when I was a bride.' "

To these last words the audience responded with deep silence. Ingrid and Esther then sat down in the front pew. After a few moments I continued from the pulpit:

"This is love which reflects the love of Christ to his church.

"It is like looking into a mirror. When we look at Christ's love, we can see a picture of how God wants husband and wife to live together.

"When husband and wife live together according to God's will, their marriage becomes like a mirror, a reflection, of Christ's love.

"Martin Luther says: 'Marriage compels us to believe.' Amen."

I went down from the pulpit and sat beside my wife. Daniel concluded the service with the Lord's Prayer, a hymn, and the benediction.

We had time only to shake hands with the people as we left the church. Then we had to hurry to the airport.

Maurice offered to take us in his car, but Daniel insisted that we ride with Esther and him. This would give us half an hour with Esther and Daniel alone. It was decided that Maurice take Timothy, Miriam, and Fatma. To my surprise, Daniel's three-year-old son, who had been in church with his mother, wanted to ride with Fatma. They had become inseparable friends.

I had already climbed with Ingrid into the back seat of Daniel's car when Fatma knocked at the side window. I opened it and she handed me a thick, sealed envelope.

"Please read it before we separate," she said, then turned and went to Maurice's car.

It was addressed to both of us. So I handed it to Ingrid to read first.

"How was the sermon I missed?" she asked Daniel while opening the envelope. Evidently she didn't think the letter contained anything important.

"To me," Daniel replied as he started the car, "the sermon meant that any marriage counseling which excludes the spiritual dimension is inadequate because it does not grasp the true nature of marriage." Then he added: "It's too bad you can't stay longer."

"I'm sorry too, Daniel," I said. "We wish we could stay longer. But we have ten days of teaching together at our next stop, and the first lecture begins already this evening. There'll be about fifty key couples attending, and we'll have classes in the morning and afternoon too. The four days here were squeezed in after I got your good letter inviting us to come. Nor could we leave earlier because of our children. To have our children suffer because of our work in Family Life Seminars would really be a paradox."

"We understand," Esther said. "Please thank your children that they let you go."

"We'll do that," I answered. Then I realized that Ingrid wasn't following our conversation. I saw from her face that she was deeply moved by what she was reading. Silently, she handed me the first page. From then on we didn't speak any more until we reached the airport. Fatma was exposing all her past life before us and in the presence of God.

The letter began: "During the past days I have seen my life for the first time in the light of God's eyes. I see now that all I did was wrong, completely wrong. I forgot God. I went my own way. The most important thing in my life was not God, but myself. That's why my whole life is a mess."

A detailed description of her life story followed. It was as I had thought: she was constantly searching for a place without ever finding one.

When her father refused to let her marry her first suitor, she eloped with him far away from her home village. Her father tried to get her to return home, but she stubbornly refused. The legal status of her relationship to this man was not quite clear. She put it this way: "I got married to him by myself without God."

After she had lived with him for some months she discovered that he already had a child with another woman. In the meantime, she was pregnant and did not dare to leave him.

The next paragraph was an example of what a hell marriage can be. Nothing was omitted—distrust, quarrels, beatings, unfaithfulness. "I started to smoke pot, drink, and go to witchdoctors and fortunetellers."

Finally she left the man, but he kept her son. She chased from village to village, town to town, always looking for a place, until she ended up in this city. She couldn't even remember all the men she had lived with before John took her in.

The letter ended: "I do not blame these men. I take all the blame on myself. Consciously I transgressed all of God's commandments. I disobeyed my parents and deceived them. I am an adulteress and a murderess. I killed my baby and wanted to kill myself. I know that I have deserved God's punishment.

"But I ask God for forgiveness. I cannot set myself free in my own strength. But I trust that Christ died for me too so that I can live for him. I want to make a new start.

"Please help me to build my tent."

We had just finished Fatma's letter when we arrived at the airport. Maurice had gotten there before we did. Miriam had already gone into the terminal because she was on duty. Fatma was standing between Maurice and Timothy, turning her head in embarrassment when she saw us.

Daniel parked beside Maurice's car. Ingrid stepped out and gave Fatma a warm, sisterly hug. Then Fatma broke down, put her head on Ingrid's shoulder, and cried without restraint.

"How much time do we have?" I asked Daniel.

"It's already eleven. In about half an hour they will call your flight."

"All right. Let's continue our teamwork, Daniel, even in the last hour of our stay. Here are our tickets. Could Maurice and Timothy check our big suitcases? And could you and Esther take our hand baggage and give it to us at the gate?"

While the others went to the counter with our baggage, Ingrid and I took Fatma between us and went to the waiting room. It was full of people and very noisy. We found three armchairs in a row.

"Are you shocked, Pastor?" Fatma asked.

"No, I am happy."

"Happy?"

"Yes, because there is great joy in heaven over one sinner who repents."

Fatma seemed relieved that we did not condemn her. "Do you think I can be forgiven?" she asked.

"Yes," I answered. "But first you must realize that you didn't write the letter to us but to God. We are only your witnesses."

"Yes, I know that."

"Are you willing to accept our word of forgiveness as God's word of forgiveness?"

"Yes, I am."

"Then please read the last paragraph of your letter again." I handed her the envelope and she unfolded the letter on her lap.

"I want to start a little before the last paragraph," she said.

She read in a half-loud voice, pronouncing every word distinctly: ". . . I transgressed all of God's commandments. I disobeyed my parents and deceived them. I am an adulteress and a murderess. I killed my baby . . ."

Her voice choked. She sobbed and her whole body shook. "Do you understand that I killed a life?" she cried. "Abortion is murder, regardless of what they say. How can I ever make that good again?"

Ingrid put her left arm around Fatma's shoulder and said: "Fatma, there are things we can never make right again. We can only place them under the cross."

At that Fatma was calmed and could continue to read: "I . . . wanted to kill myself. I know that I have deserved God's punishment. But I ask God for forgiveness. I cannot set myself free in my own strength. But I trust that Christ died for me too so that I can live for him. I want to make a new start. Please help me to build my tent."

Fatma put the letter back in the envelope. She placed it on her lap, covering it with her folded hands. She closed her eyes and bowed her head slightly. I knew that she was praying.

It was a strange situation. People were rushing by. Some were watching us, not knowing what to think. The loudspeaker announced constantly arriving and departing planes.

But we forgot all those around us. We were in God's presence. He's not only in churches. He's at airports as well.

I put my left hand over Fatma's folded hands and Ingrid put her right hand on top, leaving her left arm protectingly around Fatma's shoulders.

I said: "Lord, I thank you that you have forgiven me my sins and that I can now pass on what I have received."

Then I placed my right hand on Fatma's head and said:

"Thus says the Lord: Fatma, fear not. Fatma, I have redeemed you. Fatma, I have called you by name. Fatma, you are mine. Though your sins are like scarlet, they shall be as white as snow; though they are red like crimson, they shall become like wool. Take heart, Fatma; your sins are forgiven. Go, and do not sin again. Everyone who commits sin is a slave to sin. If the Son makes you free, you will be free indeed."*

Ingrid added: "I want to give you Jeremiah 3:14 in a very personal form, Fatma: Return, O faithless child, says the Lord, for I married you."

Without moving, Fatma sat with closed eyes. Her body was trembling slightly. Then she said:

"I'm in God's tent now, am I not?"

"Yes, this is your place. As Ingrid said, God married you."

"I shall get my things from John's house tonight," she said.

* Isa. 43:1, 1:18; Matt. 9:2; John 8:11, 34, 36.

"Take Esther along."

"I will. I shall stay with her for the next few weeks. She told me what you said about a place. Daniel will try to find one for me."

Our flight was being called over the loudspeaker.

"Just two more things, Fatma," I said. "First, you are free now, absolutely free. The past is effaced from God's memory. If you continue to burden yourself with your forgiven sins, you commit a new one."

"I understand."

"Second, the grace of God is like a growing light which falls into a dark room. But this is a process which goes on and on. It may well be that during the next days you will discover still more dark things in your life which you could not see today. Do not be depressed and desperate if you do. It means simply that your life is exposed to the light of God."

"Thank you."

Daniel came rushing toward us: "You have to come right away. Here are your boarding cards. People are already getting on the plane and you haven't even gone through the passport control yet."

"But they just called our flight."

"That was the second call. You didn't hear the first one."

We got up and followed Daniel as quickly as possible. Fatma stood with Ingrid as I gave the official our passports to be stamped.

"How do you feel, Fatma?" Ingrid asked.

She thought for a moment and then she said: "Strange, I'm alone and still I don't feel lonesome."

"That's just the point. I believe that only those should marry who are able to live alone. God wants you to prove yourself."

I gave Ingrid her passport and we dashed to the gate where Miriam was checking the boarding cards.

Esther and Daniel gave us our hand baggage. Now we had no hands free, so our friends hugged us warmly.

"God used you both," Daniel said.

"In spite of ourselves," I answered.

As I turned to say good-by to Maurice, I remembered that he still wanted to ask me a question.

"Please write your question to me," I said.

"I've done that already," he answered, thrusting an envelope into my jacket pocket.

We passed through the gate, leaving the others behind. Miriam was the only one allowed to accompany us to the plane.

In her usual directness, she asked: "Do you remember my first letter to you when I wrote you that I was afraid that my feelings for Timothy were not quite deep enough for marriage? And you told me I should listen to my feelings, because girls usually feel it sooner than boys. Now what I'm wondering is, when things work out, is it also the girl who feels it before the young man?"

"What do you think, Miriam?"

She didn't reply immediately. When we were halfway up the landing stairs, she called out:

"I'm sure she does!"

I could only wave at her in approval. We were the last ones to enter the plane. The stewardess was already closing the door as we took our places beside each other and fastened our seatbelts. Before long the plane started to move and taxied out to the runway.

Ingrid put her hand over mine.

"I'm sorry and ashamed about this morning," she said. "Sometimes I just have the feeling I can't quite keep in stride with you. Do you understand?"

"It was a good way to keep us humble," I replied. "I think God lets us go through these valleys in order that we understand the problems of other couples better."

The plane was now racing for the takeoff. The concrete of the runway disappeared. The earth moved away. The plane headed into the open sky.

We were on our way again—*unterwegs,* en route.

"Why don't you open Maurice's letter?" Ingrid asked.

"What do you think is in it—another confession?"

"I have a feeling it's something else."

"What makes you think so? Feminine intuition?"

"Yes."

"Tell me before I open it."

"Didn't you notice how happy Maurice was when it was decided that Fatma ride with him to the airport?"

"You mean . . . ?"

"Open it and see."

I hadn't even thought of that. I tore the envelope open and read:

"Is God also a matchmaker? When I prayed in the car on the bridge while you were talking to Fatma, a voice came to me as clear as a bell: 'This girl with whom Walter is talking will be your wife.'

"It was crazy. I had never seen her before, had no idea who she was, what she looked like. I could only see her figure vaguely in the darkness.

"Could this voice be God's voice? Please send me a telegram Yes or No from your next stop."

"You and your feminine intuition!" I said to my wife with envy.

"That wasn't hard," she said.

"Poor Maurice," I muttered. "He wanted so much to marry a virgin. And he ends up with Fatma."

Ingrid contradicted me: "But she is a virgin, Walter. She's cleansed —as the bride of Christ. 'Without spot. Without wrinkle. Without blemish.' "

Indeed, Ingrid was right.

I called the stewardess and asked her whether the pilot was still in radio contact with the tower.

"Yes," she said, "but not for private messages."

"I have a very important message to an employee of your airline."

She promised to try. I gave her Miriam's name and said: "Here's the message. Just three words: 'Tell Maurice Yes.' "

Silently we sat together. Then Ingrid turned her head and looked at me.

"What's on your mind?" I asked her.

"I'm glad I married you," she said with a smile.

"So am I."